DEVILS, NOT MEN

The History of the French Foreign Legion

ROY C. ANDERSON

ROBERT HALE · LONDON

Robert Hale Limited
Clerkenwell House
Clerkenwell Green
London EC1R 0HT

British Library Cataloguing in Publication Data

Anderson, Roy
  Devils, not men – the history of the French
  Foreign Legion.
  1. France Armée Légion étrangere
  History
  I. Title
  355.3′5

  ISBN 0-7090-2946-2

Photoset in North Wales by
Derek Doyle & Associates, Mold, Clwyd.
Printed in Great Britain by
St Edmundsbury Press, Bury St Edmunds, Suffolk.
Bound by WBC Bookbinders Limited.

DEVILS, NOT MEN

Contents

Foreword

Over the long years of the French Foreign Legion's existence literally hundreds of books have been written about this unique, well-known but little understood force; of these many books nearly all have blended a great deal of fiction with fact in order to heighten the aura of aloof mystery and to titillate the reading public's vicarious appetite for thrills. Fortunately, every now and again an author will approach the subject seriously, research his matter with care, and produce an accurate and factual history – which sets the record straight for the next few years.

Roy Anderson's concise history of the Legion from its troubled beginnings as a political expediency in 1831 leads the reader through its successes and failures, portrays some of the pressures from which it has repeatedly suffered and brings him to its present state as a modern, highly sophisticated, totally integrated and vital element of France's fighting forces.

The author has taken the trouble not only to conduct his research with care but also to develop a feeling for his subject and its many facets; he has talked with and more importantly listened to legionnaires and ex-legionnaires and has, as a result, managed to identify what is important to the Legion as a whole and to legionnaires as individuals. He understands what motivates them and why and what is the antithesis of the Legion ideal. In his first chapter he sets out the Legion's ground rules: '... no man is forced to join – it is a free choice – and whatever the pressures on them afterwards, and they may be great, he has a contract to honour. If he fails to do so, other legionnaires will consider him dishonourable, at best a coward and at worst a liar, cheat and coward.' Roy Anderson has grasped what every legionnaire has always known. If the legionnaire honours his contract he is and will always be a legionnaire.

This blend of sympathetic understanding and an attention to factual detail has resulted in a work which has a firm place on the bookshelves of all students and admirers of the French Foreign Legion.

Colonel Antony Hunter-Choat,
President of the Foreign Legion Association

List of Illustrations

PICTURE CREDITS

The following photographs have been reproduced by kind permission
of: BBC Hulton Picture Library: 1, 2, 3, 8, 9; Ray Davison: 28, 32, 33,
39, 41, 48; ECPA (Photo Cinéma Vidéo des Armées): 4, 5, 6, 7, 10,
14, 17, 18, 19, 20, 21, 22, 23, 24, 25, 26, 27, 34, 38, 40, 42, 43, 44, 45,
46; Roger Viollet: 13, 16, 31; James Williamson: 11, 12; Foreign
Legion Association: 15, 29, 30, 35, 36, 37.

List of Maps

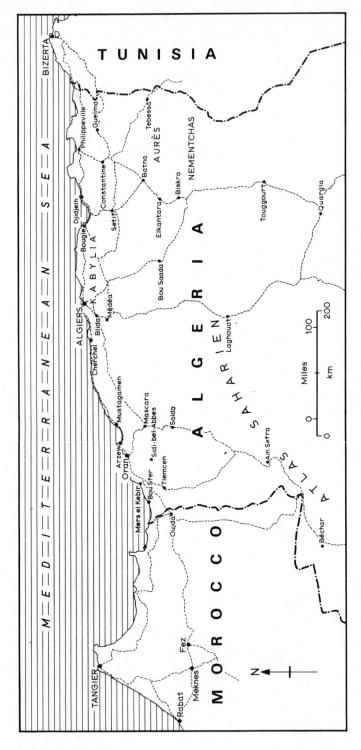

The Magrheb

Introduction

That the life of a legionnaire is hard should not be doubted, but it is not a 'hell on earth', and indeed a former British legionnaire described his service to me as 'exciting with a lot of cameraderie and fun'. But the British have long had a 'love-hate' relationship with the Legion, and anything to its disadvantage seems to be believed, whereas the achievements, particularly in regard to construction, are not so well known.

With a history dating back to 1831, the Legion is a unique formation, and it has become an international institution, although its character seems to have changed since the return from Algeria to France. Assimilation into French Army formations and the establishment of bases in metropolitan France have necessitated a new approach from the centre not only in relation to its role but in its lifestyle.

When I went to Aubagne to undertake my researches, I travelled on the boat-train from Victoria in the footsteps of many who have undertaken a similar journey in order to enlist. At Marseilles I walked beside the Old Port to the Information and Recruitment Centre, which is located at the Bas Fort St-Nicholas. Outside there is a plaque on the wall in the Legion's colours of red and green with white lettering announcing:

LEGION ETRANGERE
OUVERT JOUR ET NUIT
SONNEZ ICI

(Foreign Legion. Open day and night. Ring here.) For those who wish to re-consider their position before entering, there is a nearby coffee cabin!

So began my first visual contact with the Legion about which I had read and of which I had heard from former legionnaires, to whom I owe a great deal; in particular Colonel Antony Hunter-Choat and John Yeowell, respectively President and Secretary of the British (former) Foreign Legionnaires Association, and Jim Worden, who served with the 3rd REI and the 2nd REP. James Williamson, who joined the Legion in 1937 and served at Narvik, gave me much graphic detail of this campaign. There have been many links in various chains but without the permission of the French Ministry of Defence and the authorization to consult the Legion's archives given by Lieutenant-Colonel Jean-Richard (to whom Colonel Romain-Desfosses, National President of the National Union of Parachutists wrote on my behalf), I believe this book would have been less than adequate.

This authority brought forth the help of Lieutenant-Colonel Chiaroni and Warrant Officer J. Cuba (the curator of the Legion's museum at Aubagne), who made me most welcome at Aubagne, patiently dealing with all my queries and making much information available to me, particularly in relation to the post-Algerian years of the Legion. Mark Milburn suggested several lines of enquiry, and his assistance has been invaluable. Ann Crook typed the manuscript, and to her I express my thanks not only for her expertise but for the interest she has shown in the work.

In the text 'legionnaire' refers to all members of the Legion, regardless of rank. A comparative table of ranks is set out in Appendix 3, but exact equivalents do not always exist. Regimental and formation titles are given in English translation (but with initials of the French name, which may be found in Appendix 3), except where there is no exact translation in which case the French is used.

My own service experience was gained in the Royal Air Force, and this gave me standards against which to test my observations. All the opinions are mine. It has been a most absorbing history to research, leaving me with unqualified admiration for the Legion and the legionnaires.

R.C. Anderson
Manaton, Devon

1 Légionnaire

Despite two world wars, Indo-China, Algeria and Kolwezi, the popular impression of the *Légion Etrangère* (French Foreign Legion) still held by many Britons is that it provides a haven for unrequited lovers or those distancing themselves from a scandal of which they are improperly accused or suspected. The reality of the Legion, however, is hard work and harsh discipline, and when it comes to combat, the lot of the legionnaire has not greatly changed since General François de Négrier (one of the Legion's most famous commanding officers) told them in 1883, 'You legionnaires are soldiers in order to die, and I am sending you where you can die.'

As a fighting force, the Legion has always been exceptionally valiant, often suffering heavy casualties in securing their objectives, and whilst there is no reason to believe that its officers have deliberately sought a big 'butcher's bill', there is no doubt that their audacious tactics, discipline and bravery have often resulted in victories where larger concentrations of troops have failed. A particular case was the conflict in Indo-China in the early 1950s when the Legion provided twenty per cent of the maintained troops but suffered forty-eight per cent of the total casualties. Training and discipline have always been harsh and, although somewhat tempered today as a result of social changes, they remain significantly tougher than in national armies. On the other hand, the Legion has a strict code of honour in regard to its casualties and does not abandon its dead on the field of battle: '*La Légion n'abandonne pas ses morts.*'

In the mountains of North Africa, extremes of weather, primitive conditions of living, and fighting often in desperate situations, where no quarter was given by either side, brought about a system of control exercised by arbitary and brutal discipline. At Saida, for instance, in the mid-thirties, a notice was displayed on the entrance to the punishment cells which read, 'You enter like a lion and leave like a lamb.' Saida had been the old base of the 3rd Foreign Infantry Regiment (3rd REI) and earlier still a controlled fort of the 2nd REI. Similar measures were necessary to combat periods of boredom in isolated forts, and so evolved the Legion's great history of construction.

There does appear to have been and still to be a gulf between officers and legionnaires, but senior NCOs probably have much greater influence than junior officers. However, all accounts of the Legion confirm that the more senior rank held by an officer, the greater affection and admiration he has for those under his command, but whilst many of the senior commanders have inspired legionnaires to great acts of bravery, as individuals these same officers may not have been particularly popular.

So high is the esteem of the Legion that only the top six entrants who pass out at St-Cyr (the French equivalent of Sandhurst) are given the opportunity of serving with the Legion, so they consider it an honour to do so – but they do not necessarily become legionnaires. General de Gaulle never made it but General Koenig did, wearing on the sleeve of his jacket the stripes of both a *caporal chef** of the Legion and a *brigadier chef* of the Cavalry. It is thought that he is the only officer to have achieved this distinction except for General Rollet, 'Father of the Legion'. Indeed, it is easier for an officer to become a general than to become an honorary *caporal chef* in the Legion, and any officer fortunate enough to be so honoured will wear the badge of Legionnaire with great pride.

Over the years the Legion has attracted all manner of persons into its ranks. There have been officers and other ranks from national armies; titled persons, including princes and dukes; priests, doctors and professional men from all walks of life, right down to a category described by the Duke of Wellington of his troops before Waterloo as 'the scum of the earth'. Whilst some joined for a love of adventure, or for patriotic reasons in war time, others just wished to fight and considered that the Legion would give them the best opportunity. For many the Legion has been seen as an escape – one who did escape into it was Mussolini's physician, who enlisted after World War II and became an *adjudant chef médic*.

In many conflicts the Legion's involvement has been in situations

---

* For translation of Legion ranks, which do not always have a British equivalent, see Appendix 3.

where most of the legionnaires had no personal motive for fighting, apart from their own survival, so, for them, at the conclusion, there was no return to their homeland, ensuring no triumphal welcome from grateful civilians. Adrian Liddell Hart (who served with the Legion in Indo-China) commented that some of the prejudice directed against the Legion is prompted by the inference that many legionnaires are willing to fight and die bravely for the sake of war itself, not necessarily inspired by love of wives and families, faith or country. For this reason I am indebted to a former British *caporal chef* of the Legion (who wishes to remain anonymous) who maintains that courage and bravery are like a disease: they are contagious and are handed down to inheritors and successors in the 'traditions'. But good leaders are also required, because cowardice is also contagious.

It is, however, the author's conclusion that the legionnaires make the Legion, bringing to it their national characteristics and what appears to be an almost unlimited range of professional and technical skills that they harness to the Legion's interests.

In the field of conflict the Legion gives certain definite awards for brave conduct. In particular the system of promotion under fire and the award of the Military Medal or the Croix de Guerre not only bring with them honour but also firm rewards in terms of leave. Whatever the Legion authorities may say, there is a certain notoriety in serving with it, and the mystique is quietly cultivated. Accounts are regularly given to the legionnaires, particularly in training, of the heroic actions of their predecessors, and there is evidence to suggest that many legionnaires react so positively that there are even instances of legionnaires throwing themselves in front of their officers to protect them from enemy bullets. Accounts suggest that legionnaires always tend to fight best when encircled, cut off or faced with great odds – situations which their training would appear to fit them for, particularly the art of self-survival related to the individual's performance in his own group. Perhaps some of the valour of the legionnaires is a result of their very reason for joining: their desperation or 'couldn't care less' attitude to life that brings to the fore bravery, underpinned by confidence in their training and professionalism.

Whilst in theory the different nationalities in the Legion are not recognized, national characteristics are utilized: Germans have always been regarded as well disciplined and tenacious, with the

Spaniards possessing great skills in 'hand-to-hand' fighting, whilst the French are most effective in small groups where gallantry with a certain amount of panache brings out the best in them. The British, with notable exceptions, have not made a great impression on the Legion, possibly because until recent years only a relatively small number served. This produces an unfair comparison – although the Legion's view is that a good British legionnaire is 'very good'. Today the situation is somewhat different. A recently discharged legionnaire commented that, in his section, thirty-two were English-speaking, eight German or Dutch and six French. The Germans still form an important nucleus of the Legion, and without them the French would have quite a problem to maintain the Legion's fighting efficiency. So building on the inherent national characteristic and fusing them together brings out a unique set of abilities that can be put to very good use in combat.

The fact that many legionnaires have held commissioned or NCO rank in national armies must give a great advantage in difficult situations, when legionnaires experienced in leadership can, if necessary, take over command.

There are those who look upon the Legion as a military monastic order, and the very fact that a man can break with the past and make a new start is part of the myth of our civilization. The Legion is a symbol of French glory and has great prestige on account of its efficiency and valour and the fact that it is a unique embodiment of the French military tradition, the officers of today being descended from those who led the foreign mercenaries under the old French monarchy that helped to make France the greatest military power in Europe. The Legion is an invaluable force which the French have had at their command for over 150 years and which they have deployed in very disagreeable situations where French public opinion could not accept the use of the national army. The brutal truth is that the French have always considered the legionnaires expendable, and the ironic circumstances of their recruiting many ex-Wehrmacht and SS troops at the end of World War II for service in the Legion in Indo-China indicates recognition of expediency. In the early 1950s these actions brought a very strong backlash led by the Social Democrats in the Federal Republic of Germany, particularly in relation to tactless incidents where bus-loads of recruits were rushed across the frontier despite the protests of the German police.

Until 1962 all recruits received a medical examination and signed their provisional contracts at the recruiting centres before transferring to Fort St-Jean (later the Bas-Fort St-Nicholas) at Marseilles, where they embarked for Algeria. For the journey they received a motley collection of cast-off uniform clothing, their civilian clothes being auctioned off to dealers. Until 1960 initial kitting out took place at Sidi-bel-Abbès; after that at Marseilles. Security checks by the Deuxième Bureau (the French military intelligence service) were of necessity completed before a recruit left France. In post-war years the security and medical checks have become progressively more rigorous.

All these actions resulted from the Legion's policy of divesting the recruit of his civilian status. Under French law, the Legion is entitled to deny the existence of an individual in its ranks, and anyone who betrays the professional secret is liable to be prosecuted under the Penal Code of the French Republic. However, a Ministerial Directive of 1931 provided that, before such refusal could be made, commanding officers are required to interview the man concerned as to whether or not he has any information to be divulged. It is also considered an anti-social act in the Legion to put the question to another legionnaire, although there are those who themselves declare their reasons for joining.

Although the initial selection, cursory medical examination and signing of provisional contracts still take place at the recruiting centres, entrants are now despatched to the Legion's headquarters at the Quartier Viénot, Aubagne, where the final choice is made from the hundreds who offer their services – in 1984, of the 6,000 who applied only 1,300 were accepted. It is important to emphasize again that no man is forced to join – it is a free choice – and whatever the pressures on them afterwards, and they may be great, he has a contract to honour. If he fails to do so, other legionnaires will consider him dishonourable, at best a coward and at worst a liar, cheat and coward. When the Legion was in Algeria, the very physical circumstances of its units and the difficulty in deserting to a friendly power placed certain advantages in the hands of the authorities, and Arabs who captured and returned a deserter received a bounty of 200 francs – a large sum in the 1930s. Today, with the majority of legionnaires based in mainland France, maintaining this level of control is more difficult, particularly as travel between countries is so much easier. In fact, it is whispered that, if a legionnaire has his identity card and a return ticket, travel between European countries and Britain is 'no problem', immigration authorities permitting such travel.

The prospect of stiff penalties upon recapture does not appear to prevent a high level of desertion, although there is 'desertion and desertion'. A legionnaire who goes AWOL for a couple of days and returns to his regiment can expect eight days extra duty. However, all military personnel who quit the limits of French territory without authorization are considered deserters (even for twenty-four hours), though a man of advancing years, recaptured after sixteen years 'on the run', received only six months imprisonment and was then discharged. Others have not been so lucky, and a legionnaire who had been away for eighteen years who was arrested for a minor traffic offence was required to complete his service after a period of imprisonment. In fact, any legionnaire who deserts to his home country and subsequently returns to France can expect at the very least to be required to honour his five-year contract. A man deserting with a weapon is a potential murderer, and in the Legion it is considered right and proper that he be shot before having the opportunity to use his weapon on defenceless civilians.

For those who have only recently enlisted, the penalty for desertion is relatively modest insofar as the French Code of Military Justice provides that, until a man has completed three months service, he will not be posted as a deserter until his absence exceeds one month. Upon return to the centre the likely punishment is eight days extra duty. If the absence occurs whilst he is travelling between one corps and another or is on leave, he will be considered a deserter only fifteen days after the date fixed for his arrival. Again, the basic punishment is 'eight days', plus an extra day for each day's absence.

With unemployment running high in Europe, the Legion can hand- pick its new recruits, and whilst a man may still enlist under an assumed name, the Deuxième Bureau and Interpol check him out to ensure that he is not a wanted murderer or perhaps an international terrorist. The Legion will nevertheless accept certain petty criminals and minor offenders into its ranks because it is certainly not a force for those who are looking for an easy life, and tough men are preferred. Once a man has committed himself to the five-year contract of service, there is no going back, but if the Legion does not want him for any reason, he will be quietly shown the door within the initial selection period (or, exceptionally, if he is found unsuitable during training), and if he is being sought for a major crime, it could well be that the authorities will be waiting for him outside the gate. One legionnaire explained that, when he went into the recruiting centre to obtain information, no one spoke English, and he found himself signing a document in French (all documentation is in French) which meant he had joined!

During the three-week selection period at Aubagne, potential recruits are graded by colours: yellow after they have survived the first week, green for the second, and red for the third and final week, which indicates the man is 'clean' and can be accepted into the Legion's ranks. The check and medical examinations become more intensive as the selection period progresses, until the new entrant is finally chosen to begin his training as part of the five-year contract. This system of checking surprises many new entrants nurtured on the idea that the Legion will accept anyone, irrespective of background or abilities. So deep-rooted is this view that it was stated by the defending counsel at the Old Bailey, London, in August 1983, on behalf of a Briton who had committed a crime, joined the Legion, deserted and given himself up to the British authorities: 'He knew no questions would be asked of him about his past.'

No particular discipline is exacted in this period: the men are rather left to themselves, and there are fights and quarrels, but any recruit found in possession of a personal weapon is likely to be summarily and savagely beaten by the NCOs. However, it would seem that the recruits' conduct is quietly observed, as this is an important ingredient in assimilation. Although there has been some variation over the years, the present practice is that civilian clothes must then be handed over, for which the legionnaire receives 200 francs – the clothes being given to the Red Cross.

The new recruits, known as *engagés volontaires* (or '*les Bleus*' – 'the Blues') are made up into groups of thirty, then assembled and, complete with their kit, transferred to the training regiment, the 4th Foreign Regiment (4th RE) at Castelnaudary, based at the Quartier Lapasset. There are still those who join the Legion because they consider it romantic. Perhaps they have read a book or heard stories, many of which are escapes from reality. Upon arriving at Castelnaudary, this image will soon be shattered.

Approximately 350 recruits are in training at any time, controlled by a staff of thirty-five officers and 120 NCOs. (An interesting variation from British military procedure is that, besides commissioned officers, it is also necessary to salute NCOs.) The initial training lasts for fifteen weeks and is very hard, not only in respect of the exercises but in the level of discipline which is maintained. Tales of actual physical assault upon new recruits appear to be exaggerated, and whilst a traditional 'kick up the backside' may well take place, the quickest way for a sergeant to lose his stripes is to strike a recruit. In fact, the old 'rule of brutality' was abolished in 1925, when General Rollet instituted a code of conduct making such action a serious offence. However, a legionnaire has the right to request 'individual contest' against a corporal or sergeant instructor. Recruits are not allowed out of camp for the first two months of their training and, should they have occasion to leave camp for training exercises or construction work during this period, they are generally guarded by armed NCOs. The Legion would suggest that the weapon is to guard the novice legionnaires and constitutes authority, but the British Army, for instance, does not require such protection.

Basic training is similar to that of most other national armies, with cleaning, fatigues, arms and foot drill, singing, weapon training, lectures, French language, route marches, physical education and close combat, with punishments for infringements of the regulations. There does not appear, however, to be a training programme common to all entrants, each *chef de section* appearing to pursue his own ideas, with plenty of periods of *corvée* ('fatigues'), often for a week or two at a time. A legionnaire with previous military experience suggested to the author that there was more fatigues than training!

Punishments vary from minor confinement or extra guard duty to custodial sentences. Such time spent in custody is unpaid and does not count against the five-year contract. The Legion seems to believe that it can reform all its bad characters, and no discharges take place. If they did, there would be plenty attempting to 'work their ticket', and this is one army where it is no use trying!

There is a view in the Legion that many of the recruits expect hard treatment and are looking for a disciplined life. Certainly during the fifteen-week training period the legionnaire will get this. However, the harsh conditions of service in the Legion mean that desertion during training is not uncommon, but whether this results from the circumstances surrounding the training, the shock of entering the Legion or the realization that it is not the solution to the recruit's problems is hard to determine. Perhaps it is a combination of all. A man who becomes a legionnaire must accept the fact that one day he may be required to die for the Legion, because those who cross it in combat know that the Legion is always prepared to fight to the last man.

This fighting spirit manifests itself in the off-duty life of the legionnaire, who, if he is bored, can often be trouble. There is plenty of drinking but brawling amongst legionnaires is uncommon. In matters of brawling with 'outsiders', the Legion conducts itself according to its own principles and rules, with outside intervention by local police or other enforcement agencies not only considered unwelcome and insulting but positively discouraged, the attitude being neatly summed up in the French expression *'et ta soeur'* – 'and your sister!'

Base barrack hours are from 08.00 hours to 18.00 hours. The legionnaire has reveille at 05.30 or 06.00, work commencing within one hour. Early morning sport, or jogging for NCOs, is obligatory, and toilet, barrack room and cleaning details are all completed by 08.00. There is, however, a two-hour break at midday. In the summer months in the South of France most legionnaires 'get off camp' after duty rather than undertake 'piquet duty' which involves them in helping combat the forest fires which occur quite regularly.

After going through the induction procedure and receiving a pay advance, recruits meet their corporal. His effectiveness will probably be achieved if the men under his command hate him, but if they can also add a measure of respect, they are fortunate. However, this does not seem to be a substantially different situation from that prevailing in most national armies.

Food, cooked in the French style, is generally considered good, and coffee is served every morning (except Sunday when it is hot chocolate), together with bread, cheese, sardines or salami. The food is accompanied by a quarter litre of wine or beer (the army issue mug is called *'le quart'* because it holds a quarter litre) at each meal. Whilst food is adequate, healthy appetites mean that slow eaters go hungry, as the food is placed on the tables and not on individual plates at the servery.

There is a similarity with national armies in the barracks, which contain a particular training entry under the supervision of its officers and NCOs and where equipment and bed space must be presented in the approved manner and the recruits be available for inspection. The legionnaire of today may retain with him a few personal items on a special shelf in his locker, but space must be reserved for the white kepi, which is displayed with the crossed red epaulettes.

In earlier years the language problem was emphasized by NCOs striking those who could not immediately comprehend a command. Perhaps where life was simpler, in the terrain of North Africa, this did not present a problem, insofar as a Legion *patois* developed which covered most situations. In a modern 'intervention service' using sophisticated equipment, such a situation can no longer be tolerated, but whilst today classes are given in basic French, the amount of language training seems to be variable, depending on the attitude of the *chef de section*. The Legion has developed its own, slow method: a combination of visual aids and blackboard tuition, with students repeating words until they become proficient, enabling them to build up phrases. To some extent the Legion relies more on the buddy' system, each non-French-speaking legionnaire being allocated a French-speaking 'buddy'. This system falls into difficulty when the French are in the minority in the section. At the completion of training, the legionnaire has a test, the questions requiring answers in French, identifying photographs. Whilst some recruits have difficulty in giving satisfactory answers because of the language problem, those of normal intelligence will have a sufficient basic knowledge of French to function without being a menace.

One of the traditions of the Legion is its singing, and besides learning the basic drill movements, the recruits are also taught the songs which have been sung by their predecessors over the years, particularly '*Le Boudin*', 'The Black Pudding', whose meaning and theme have been subject to much speculation: it is thought that the 'black pudding' refers to the sausage-shaped tent roll which used to be carried across the top of the legionnaire's backpack. '*Le Boudin*', is sung on the majority of ceremonial occasions and in the officers' and NCOs' messes prior to the meal, when it is followed by a toast, '*La Poussière*' ('The Dust'), after which the glasses are traditionally upturned.

This is quite different from British military tradition, where no great regard is placed on singing and the unity it develops. Singing plays a very important part in Legion life, and whilst each regiment has its own marching songs, all the songs are sung by all regiments. It is by singing when marching without a band that the Legion is able to maintain its slow step. Most of the songs originated in Germany – the '*Képi Blanc*' ('White Kepi), for example, is sung to the melody of the World War II Panzer Division song. The song of the 2nd REI is 'Anne Marie' (words are in German), whilst that of the 3rd REI is '*Mein Regiment, Mein Heimatland*' ('My Regiment, My Homeland'), and the 1st REC sing '*Wir sind die Legionäre*' ('We are the Legionnaires). Other songs taught today are also German: '*Westerwald*', '*Kameraden*', '*Ich hatt' einen Kamerad*' ('Western Forest', 'Comrades', 'I had a Comrade'.) It is not surprising, therefore, that the Legion has a particularly accomplished band, Musique Principale de la Légion Etrangère, which consists of ninety musicians attached to the 1st RE and based at Aubagne.

The legionnaire's most treasured possession, his white kepi, is officially presented some four weeks into initial training at a torchlight ceremony, where the Major reminds the recruits of their pledge of honour and fidelity, after which they sing '*Le Boudin*' before placing the white kepi on their heads. This ceremonial is part of the development of the mystique and tradition of the Legion and again has some similarity with a religious order. Those who accept the Legion, its rules and strong disciplines enter into membership of a family to which, for instance, many stayed loyal during two world wars, whilst declining to fight against their own countrymen.

With the completion of the legionnaire's training, he is posted to one of the regiments, and specialist training commences. Unlike those of many national armies, recruits do not enlist for specific trades: they enlist as legionnaires, and it is the Legion which harnesses their skills to its needs. Commando training is undertaken at the French Army's training school at Mont Louis, close to Andorra. Here specialist training is undertaken in a number of roles in which legionnaires could be employed. Those who are posted to the Legion's elite 1st Foreign Cavalry Regiment (1st REC) will go to its depot at Orange, where they are trained in the use of the various armoured fighting vehicles used by the regiment, including the AMX 10-RC.

A regiment of the Legion which has become world-famous is the 2nd Foreign Parachute Regiment (2nd REP), which has its headquarters in Calvi, on the isle of Corsica. When the Legion was based in North Africa, basic parachute training took place at Sully (about ten miles/sixteen kilometres from Sidi-bel-Abbès) after which legionnaires went to the French Army parachute-training school at Blida to complete their training. In all its training, including the parachute course, the Legion still places great emphasis on the ability of legionnaires to march across country quickly and effectively. Route marches commence in the first two weeks of training, then every Saturday. The first march is about fifteen miles (twenty-five kilometres), after which they become progressively longer, culminating with a sixty-mile (hundred kilometres) march on a forty-eight hour exercise. The Legion has specialist mountain and small-boat units and is maintained at constant readiness for action, wherever it may be required.

What then can a trained legionnaire expect during this five-year contract? This will, of course, depend largely on where he is posted, the country's requirements and the duties to be performed. Those on detachment in Guyane (French Guyana), which the French have been using in recent years for the firing of the European rocket Ariane, will have a life very different from that at headquarters in Aubagne or at one of the regimental depots.

Sports facilities are provided, and off-duty the legionnaire will be allowed to leave camp to enjoy whatever facilities are available in the locality – but not in civilian clothes. Uniform is worn at all times. Civilian clothes are allowed only to those legionnaires who have been accorded '*rectification d'état civile*', certifying that the name adopted in the Legion is their true name, with documentation to prove it. Even NCOs require '*rectification*' to wear civilian clothes, and only after three years' service.

Each camp has its open mess, knows as the '*foyer*', where there is much drinking and singing, and even today each regiment of the Legion discreetly maintains its '*Bordel Militaire Contrôlé*, the military brothel. In fact, the BMC always accompanied the regiment even on missions away from the base. The girls are paid but records are kept of the events so that the auditor of the brothel can claim ten per cent for Legion funds. Each brothel has its bar and is a place of recreation insofar as legionnaires who visit it are not obliged to take part in the sexual activities.

Leave – '*permission*' – with freedom of movement is a privilege now enjoyed by legionnaires, although in some areas they will be allowed to go only to the Legion's rest camps. In Marseilles the

Legion maintains its own hotel. There is full freedom of movement throughout France, and legionnaires receive seventy-five per cent off SNCF rail fares. In fact, the scale of allowance is ten days in the first year, fifteen days per annum thereafter. If, however, at the end of his five-year contract the legionnaire has not taken leave, he will be authorized ninety days. A legionnaire is not allowed to marry during the initial five-year contract, but if he enlists for a further period, he may obtain permission to marry. Contrary to popular belief, comfortable quarters are provided for families. As in many other European armies, marriage allowances are paid, rents are modest and family functions arranged. In particular, the Fête de Camerone (Camerone Day) is considered a great family day in the Legion, when there are parties, games and food fit for a gourmet, as well as parades.

Christmas is one of the Legion's most important feasts of the year. After Midnight Mass there is Christmas dinner – but this is an event reserved for the legionnaires, not their families. Every legionnaire receives from the Company Commander a personally chosen Christmas gift, and this once again underlines the family spirit of the Legion. These gifts are purchased from the accumulated profits of the '*foyer*', brothel, officers' mess and NCOs' mess. The fund is also responsible for buying presents for all children of legionnaires – including the officers'.

On Easter Day officers and their wives visit the refectory at lunchtime to distribute eggs, hot cross buns and cigarettes.

On New Year's Day the senior NCOs entertain the officers in their mess, and on the Feast of Epiphany (6 January) the officers return the compliment. In addition each regiment has its own commemorative day when significant events are remembered, one of the best-known being the Fête de la Fourragère (Lanyard Festival) which takes place on 14 September in the 3rd Foreign Infantry Regiment (3rd REI), to which old comrades of the Foreign Legion Marching Regiment (RMLE) are invited.

It is possible for a legionnaire to become a senior NCO within ten years. Should he decide to leave the Legion at that time, he can elect to become a French citizen. Commissioning is a possibility from the ranks, but the position is that only ten per cent of the officers are non-French, although commissioned officers from national armies can serve with the Legion provided their Government is agreeable. At the conclusion of fifteen years' service, each legionnaire will be entitled to a small pension; after twenty years it is considerably better, and many men re-enlist for the additional period to obtain the increased benefit. At the time of writing (August 1985), basic pay for a recruit is about 1,900 francs each month and the average pay for a Corporal with less than five years' service is £600 per month. All legionnaires receive 30 francs per day 'field pay'. A legionnaire serving in the 2nd REP would receive additional cash, 'jump' pay, on completion of the required annual number of jumps. Overseas pay can again increase the earnings of a legionnaire: one serving in Djibouti can expect to receive something in the region of 8,000 francs a month. Fifty years ago a man received a bounty of 500 francs when he enlisted, and a franc a day thereafter, at a time when the exchange range was about 100 francs to the pound.

For the veteran legionnaires, there is the Domaine Capitaine Danjou (Captain Danjou Estate), a home which accommodates 180 pensioners who are cared for by the Legion in old age. This is situated in the South of France, to the west of St-Maximin in the village of Puyloubier. Here the Legion has its own vineyard, and many of the more active pensioners enjoy a day's work there or in the small craft industries where souvenirs are made for sale in the Legion's gift-shops. On Camerone Day, they honour the memory of their former comrades either at the Legion's memorial in the small cemetery of Puyloubier or at the base camp at Aubagne, in company with legionnaires from the Old Comrades Association throughout the world. Legionnaires and those interested in the Legion's activities are kept in touch by the Legion's own high-quality magazine, the *Képi Blanc*, published at the headquarters in Aubagne.

Discharge from the Legion is also a matter of considerable importance, and it is known as 'the Ceremony of Liberation'. Legionnaires return to Aubagne for this parade, when they receive their official discharge certificate. At this time, after handing in their uniforms, they receive new civilian clothes from the Legion's clothing store. For the majority their days in the Legion are over, but there will be a few unable to settle in civilian life who will re-enlist.

2 The Early Years

The revolution of 25 July 1830, which drove King Charles X into exile in Britain and established the 'July Monarchy' of Louis-Philippe, was a regime not without enemies. These ranged from 'republicans' who considered themselves robbed of their revolution through to 'legitimists' of the Bourbon party, who regarded Louis-Philippe as a usurper. In addition, there were a large number of 'purged' officers and soldiers with the potential to give armed assistance to any opposition. A real stroke of luck was an unpopular year-old war in Algeria being fought by France to curb Mediterranean pirates.

It was from this unlikely combination of circumstances that on 9 March 1831 a Royal Ordinance announced the formation of a Foreign Legion to be recruited from sources outside French territory. Marshal Soult (the French Minister of War) decided that the Foreign Legion 'should not be employed in the continental territory of the kingdom'; a supplementary order of 18 March 1831 barred enlistment by Frenchmen, or married men, without special dispensation. Organization of its battalions was to be the same as for French line infantry, each battalion having eight companies of 112 men, and, so far as possible, each company was to be composed of men of the same nationality; enlistment to be voluntary for a minimum of three and a maximum of five years; men to be at least five feet (1.52 metres) tall, aged between eighteen and forty years, to be established by a birth certificate, in good health and of good character. Uniforms were also to be those of the metropolitan French line infantry, i.e. crimson trousers, royal blue tailcoat, heavy black shako (cap), and an iron-grey greatcoat carried rolled in a ticking cover on the knapsack.

In practice, recruiting-standards were liberally interpreted, so much so that, if a man appeared fit enough for military service, he was signed up. Many gaols and workhouses were emptied of 'recruits', and would-be colonialists rubbed shoulders with drunkards, criminals, ex-soldiers and all manner of characters. Many of the officers had served previously in Napoleon's *Grande Armée*, and it seems that some Frenchmen *were* recruited. Initially the depot was at Langres, then at Bar-le-Duc, and later at Toulon. As the recruits came in (with all their varied reasons for joining – hardships, political motives, quest for adventure), they were formed into battalions as follows:

1st, 2nd and 3rd Battalions, formed mainly of soldiers from the Swiss and Hohenlohe regiments.

4th Battalion, largely Spanish.

5th Battalion, largely Italians and Sardinians.

6th Battalion, Belgian and Dutch.

After some initial training, the legionnaires were shipped from Toulon to Algiers, where they established themselves in the French-held coastal enclave. Watching a draft disembark, the French author Camille Rousset wrote: 'A real masquerade. To clad this mob, which comprised of men of every age from sixteen to sixty and over, we appeared to have scraped the bottom of army supplies to procure the oldest rags. They were a bizarre sight that would have delighted a circus crowd. But, their heads high, their banner before them, their drums beating to the rhythm of the famous war chant "*La Parisienne*", they proudly paraded through the crowded city streets.'

Without proper leadership and with no clear purpose, the legionnaires quickly reverted to feuding and fighting amongst themselves. Hundreds deserted, disease was rampant, legionnaires drank their pay and then ransacked Arab liquor stores, beating up their owners in the process. In fact, work had to be found to put a stop to the root cause of the problems – inactivity, and so the Legion virtually became a labour corps used on construction projects. Discipline was also a necessity and after several attempts a tough Swiss, Colonel Stoffel, accepted the challenge of knocking them into shape, although it was not until early in 1832 that some measure of order had been established. It was the process which established the traditional harsh disciplinary measures for which the Legion became infamous. No doubt, in the circumstances, strong measures were necessary, and the former Swiss and German NCOs were proficient in carrying out the wishes of their commanding officers, in an environment where desertion meant fairly certain death. These same NCOs and a goodly number of the legionnaires who had served in the Hohenlohe regiment brought with them the tradition of the slow march, at eighty-eight paces to the minute, which was adopted by the Legion and which, except on special occasions, has necessitated their placement at the rear of any parade.

As the settling-in process of the 1st, 2nd, 3rd and 5th Battalions was continuing around Algiers, the 4th were establishing themselves at Oran, whilst the partly formed 6th (Belgian) made camp at Bône. Meanwhile the 7th (Polish) Battalion was being formed in France, but when it arrived in Algeria thirty-five men were missing by evening roll-call, then a couple of days later a whole company got drunk and beat up its officers, resulting in gaol for the battalion – and two men were court-martialled.

At the same time, the French Army was still in action against those harassing European shipping, which brought them into conflict with local tribal leaders, who themselves fought one another. There was then no such country, or area of land, known as 'Algeria', so there was no central administration which France could defeat or reach an accommodation with. The coastline was not dissimilar to certain parts of southern Europe, with fertile valleys, pine-clad hillsides and towns that were solidly built and walled for defence. The fighting was done by the French Army, and the Legion was involved in the back-breaking tasks of constructing roads and similar projects. Although there were some skirmishes after Arab hit-and-run guerrilla attacks on the work groups and timber blockhouses, it was not until 27 April 1832 that the 1st and 3rd Battalions of the Legion achieved their first victory, when they stormed the redoubts covering the approaches to the village of Maison Carrée (a stronghold of the El Ouffia tribesmen, some miles east of Algiers). On 23 May Lieutenant Cham became the first Legion officer to die in battle, when he and twenty-six men were killed in an ambush in the area.

On 1 April 1832 Colonel Combe became the commanding officer and, arriving in Africa in June, brought with him the Legion's first regimental colour, which bore on its folds the inscription 'The King of France, to the Foreign Legion'.

The skills of the Arabs became evident in battle: they were courageous and ruthless, many were mounted and pressed home their mobile hit-and-run attacks with determination. As they were highly skilled in guerrilla warfare and fighting on ground of their own choosing, it is perhaps not surprising that the 4th Battalion, composed mainly of Spaniards who had some experience of this type of fighting, were the most successful against them. One tactic they adopted was to slip under a horse's stomach and tip the rider out of his saddle whilst an accomplice was waiting to stab the victim to death as he fell to the ground.

Also in April the Legion was permitted to form two elite companies, re-designated as grenadiers, with light infantrymen in each battalion. On 22 October, when the Legion boasted an effective strength of 5,538 officers, NCOs and legionnaires, Lieutenant-General Barrois reported somewhat unfavourably on appearance and uniform after his inspection at Toulon, but a second, undertaken at Mustapha on 1 December 1833, by General d'Alton, indicated an improvement, and that by General Voriol in 1834 included comments that, 'The Legion appears to be a very fine regiment ... The sixth battalion at Bône has very regular uniforms ...'

Meanwhile the young and talented Emir of Mascara, Abd-el-Kader, was fanning the flames of the smouldering Arab resistance, and on 11 November 1832 (two days after Lieutenant-Colonel Bernelle had taken command of the Legion) he arrived at the gates of Oran at the head of some 3,000 horsemen. The battle was fought on the slopes of the Djebel Tafaraouini, which was dominated by an Arab shrine named Sidi Chabel, and after an initial charge by the mounted Arab cavalry the French counter-attacked with the riflemen on the right and the legionnaires of the 4th Battalion on the left, whose combined efforts caused Abd-el-Kader to withdraw. The next four months were quiet, but in March 1833 the 6th Battalion took part in a drive against the Ouled Yacoub and Ouled Attia to the east of Algiers; in June the 4th and 5th Battalions took Arzew, and in July they took part in the capture, and later the defence, of Mostaganem. During September columns were sent against the Hadjutes and captured Coleah.

Spain was moving towards civil war, and so the 4th (Spanish) Battalion was disbanded to meet Spanish requests for the return of the troops. It was replaced by the 7th (Polish) Battalion, who then took over the duty and the number of the old 4th. After a lull in the guerrilla war, the French negotiated with Abd-el-Kader, who shrewdly took the opportunity to further his influence through the individual tribes to such an extent that in the spring he was able to field an army of 8,000 horsemen and 4,000 on foot, many of whom had been trained by European renegades. Moving against Tlemcen, which he had bypassed, he attacked General Trezel's column of 2,500 French troops at Moulay Ishmael on 26 June 1835. Legionnaires of the 4th and 5th Battalions sacrificed themselves on the rearguard when an Arab ambush on 27-29 June sought to massacre the French on the Macta saltmarshes, where a rearguard action was being fought to enable General Trezel to turn the heavy wagons on the mountain track and enable his battered column to withdraw. Legionnaires soon learned that a wise precaution was to keep the last cartridge in their pockets.

It appears that the military hierarchy in Paris was unaware of the successes of the Legion, brought about by their improved standards of training and discipline, to such an extent that a Royal Ordinance provided for the handing over of the Legion, *en bloc*, to Spain for service in the cause of the child Queen, Isabella II, who had succeeded to the throne on the death of King Ferdinand VII. Her mother, Queen Maria Cristina was appointed Regent, but the right of succession was contested by the dead King's brother, Don Carlos, who led a savage insurrection in northern Spain. As a result, Britain, France and Portugal decided in 1834 to honour a tripartite agreement and intervene on behalf of the young Isabella. The British arrived first, landing some 12,000 troops, who established themselves near San Sebastian, but the French decided on a more economical means of support, signing over the Legion to Maria Cristina on the basis that Spain would honour their terms and conditions of service. Officers were offered the opportunity of service in Spain at half pay, but the ranks had no choice and in the event were hardly ever paid or re-supplied. Bernelle was given the local rank of *Général Maréchal de Camp* on 30 June 1835, but his constant protests to Paris regarding the condition of his men led to his being relieved of command in August 1836. However, before that occurred, he reorganized his command, mixing nationalities in new battalions, and in due course the same arrangement applied at company level, affording greater efficiency, particularly in regard to co-ordination and control brought about by having French as a common language.

On 17 August 1835 six battalions consisting of 123 officers and 4,000 legionnaires landed at Tarragona. They were first employed in small units fighting irregulars in Catalonia. A Carlist attack on an isolated outpost resulted in the capture of Second Lieutenant Durmoustier and thirty legionnaires, who refused a request to change sides and were dragged from village to village, naked and bound, with their eyes put out; mercifully they were later shot. When Captain Ferrary captured a Carlist unit, he took no prisoners. Such cruelties became commonplace and, taken in conjunction with the poor provision made by those for whom the Legion was fighting, it is small wonder that the number of desertions increased.

Another innovation introduced by Bernelle was the foundation of internal support units, an artillery unit under the command of Captain Rousselet, three squadrons of lancers and a sapper unit. On 24 April 1836 the 4th and 5th Battalions fought a victorious but costly battle at Tirapegui against odds of five to one, followed by another successful action at Zubiri on 1 August, when the day was saved by Rousselet's guns but cost the 3rd and 4th Battalions 300 dead.

On 10 November 1836 Colonel Conrad succeeded Colonel Lebeau, who had commanded the Legion since 30 August 1836. He also endeavoured to improve conditions and, despite receiving a number of replacements, could field only three weak battalions. Conrad, also given the Spanish rank of *Maréchal de Camp*, made great efforts to inspire his men, despite the continued failure of the Spanish authorities to furnish the Legion with rations, clothing and pay. Following a number of small-scale operations, the Legion was reduced to a single battalion when it lost twenty officers and 350 legionnaires on 24 May 1837, during a bloody battle at Huesca in Aragon. Why did the Legion continue to fight when they were not being fed, paid or supplied? It was their inherent loyalty that brought them to their final agony in the olive groves of Barbasto on 2 June 1837. It was here that they fought a Carlist unit of 800 Legion deserters in a murderous struggle in which Colonel Conrad was killed and his place taken by Captain Bazaine. Baron von Rahden, a German soldier watching from the Carlist side wrote: 'I have never seen, throughout my rather hectic military career, neither before nor after, a battle as bloody as the one I saw there. During the combat the soldiers recognized each other, they called each other by their own names, they questioned each other – then shot each other heartlessly.'

Old scores were settled and by nightfall the opponents had fought each other to a standstill. The Legion had died by its own hand and was left to rot for six months near Pamplona until disbanded officially on 8 December 1838. Of the 5,000 or more who fought with the Legion in Spain, only 500 survived, and of these, 400 voluntarily re-enlisted for service in Algeria with the 'new Legion'.

The French Government was soon to regret having sold the 'Old Legion' to Spain and by a Royal Ordinance of 16 December 1835 established a second Legion of one battalion, to take effect on 3 February 1836, for service in Algeria, although in the event the newly formed 7th Battalion was sent to Spain in the summer of 1836 to reinforce the 'Old Legion'. During the autumn another battalion was formed at Pau, landing in Algeria early in 1837, under the command of Battalion Commander Bedeau.

For many years anti-French feelings amongst Kabyle tribesmen had been inspired by the Bey of Constantine, which caused the French to mount an (unsuccessful) attack in 1836 on the city of Constantine which, not surprisingly, encouraged the Kabyle warriors to great endeavours in their harassment of the French. In due course four companies of the Legion were encircled during a hard-fought battle at Bougie.

During July 1837 a second battalion was formed, and contingents from it and the first battalion were used to form a *bataillon de marche** as part of an expeditionary force created to mount a new attack on Constantine. Led by Governor-General Damrémont himself, the expedition marched out of Bône at the beginning of October, establishing their base on the plateau of Koudiat-Aly. The fortified city was perched high on a rock plateau surrounded by ravines, and after an artillery barrage, the French attack commenced in foul weather on 9 October. On 12 October Damrémont was killed, but on the following day legionnaires at the head of the assault group fought their way through the breach in the city wall created by the artillery barrage. Fierce hand-to-hand fighting took place in the narrow streets, and a Legion company under the command of Captain St-Arnaud (later Marshal of France) fought its way through the casbah to the El Kantara gate.

* A special unit made up of experienced legionnaires ('marching battalion').

As night fell, victory went to the French when Sergeant-Major
Doze of the Legion captured the last enemy flag (which today is
displayed at Les Invalides in Paris) and a Legion battalion
remained as part of the garrison. By December 1837 a third
battalion had been formed, bringing the Legion's strength to 3,000
men based at Algiers, Bône (now known as Annaba) and
Constantine. Scattered battles continued to be fought throughout
1838, but it was not until 1839 that any serious fighting took place,
when in May the 1st Battalion distinguished themselves at the
capture of Djidjelli.

The negotiations which took place after the fighting with
Abd-el-Kader in 1834 resulted in the Treaty of Tafna, but in
November 1839 he broke it and sent his army of 60,000 men out
into the pacified areas, slaughtering and burning the small
communities of colonialists who had established themselves under
the protection of the Legion, who responded with characteristic
ferocity and high cost. After capturing Medea and Miliana in the
spring of 1840, the 4th Battalion were besieged as they garrisoned
Miliana, and although they survived the series of attacks which
lasted from 15 June to 5 October, conditions were such that men
ran amok, attacking their comrades; one legionnaire dug his own
grave; others sat motionless, unaware of their surroundings.
Captain Bazaine asked if the surgeon could treat this madness. 'It's
not in my book,' he replied. 'Know what they call it? *Le Cafard.*'
Such was the mental state of the legionnaires that they believed a
cafard – a black beetle – had invaded their bodies and was gnawing
at their minds. So began the myth of the *cafard*, the beetle which
legionnaires blame for everything from drunkenness to murder and
desertion. In Miliana, the *cafard* thrived in the heat and the crowded,
insanitary hospital wards. When a relief column arrived, it found
only 208 out of the original 750 men still able to fight. At Fondouk
the 4th and 5th Battalions were seriously depleted by disease, losing
nine officers and 207 men dead, with 240 evacuated sick. In
addition, the 2nd Battalion fought at Bougie, the 3rd Battalion at
Boufarik and Blida, the combined actions of the five battalions
resulting in the award of a flag to the 'New Legion' in recognition of
its conduct.

Despite the harsh conditions and the campaigns in which the
Legion continued to be involved, there was no shortage of
volunteers, and on 30 December 1840 a Royal Decree ordered that

the Legion be divided into two regiments, the 1st and 2nd Foreign Legion Regiments (1st and 2nd REs). The 1st RE was formed on 1 April 1841, with its operational area in the western part of the country; the 2nd RE officially came into existence on 21 April 1841 and was stationed at Bône for duties westwards towards the Kabylia highlands, and south towards Biskra, where the Sahara meets the Aurès mountains. Earlier in 1841 a new tough Governor-General, Thomas Bugeaud de la Piconnerie, had arrived in Algeria with the intention of settling matters with Abd-el-Kader once and for all. Reasoning that fighting in the country of the enemy's choice or defending garrisons against mobile columns of Arab horsemen was wrong strategy, he planned to mount surprise attacks to destroy their villages, killing their menfolk and animals – a policy that has been adopted many times since, particularly a century later in Algeria and Vietnam.

To achieve his objectives, he organized 'flying columns' replacing wagons with mules, reducing the amount of equipment and food carried to the bare minimum. Speed was essential, and this resulted in gruelling forced marches over difficult and often hilly terrain, but as the flying columns patrolled the countryside, they built roads and outposts whilst continuing to fight the warriors of Abd-el-Kader, who lost support as the policy of the Governor-General proved effective and successful. It was whilst establishing a chain of supply dumps for these flying columns that the third battalion of the 1st RE planted its flag at Sidi-bel-Abbès, about sixty miles (96 kilometres) south of Oran, and later constructed a fortified camp which was to become the Legion's home, a garrison town designed and constructed by legionnaires. In 1840 the decision was taken to establish a permanent camp at Sidi-bel-Abbès, and the first legionnaires arrived to begin work on the construction. As a result, a small village was established to house supplies and people who were attracted to the likely business available in the area. In 1845 it was decided that the camp should be the site of a fortified town. General Lamoricère, commanding officer of the Oran division, submitted his proposals to Marshal Bugeaud, who signified his approval, with the result that a Royal Ordinance of 1847 gave formal authorization for the project. In 1848 a commission chaired by Captain Prudon completed the planning stage, and construction commenced, with the Legion providing both the skilled and unskilled manpower required.

The new town was to be half military and half civil, the initial population of 431 rising quickly to 5,259 by 1859. Besides the erection of buildings, both civil and military, a farm, attractive gardens and squares (one with a bandstand) formed part of the scheme; mains water, gas and electricity were added, as were shops, a theatre, hospital and abbattoir. NCOs of the Legion were the administrators of the town in its early days, prior to the establishment of a civilian administration. Difficulties in communications led to the construction by the Legion of a railway linking Barbe-du-Tlelat with Tlemcen, via Sidi-bel-Abbès, which was opened for traffic in May 1877. Further developments of the town led to its becoming a centre for agriculture, and by 1962 it had a population of 150,000. The main reason, however, for its existence was as the headquarters of the Legion. Further camps were built at Saida, Ain Sefra, Mascara and later at Zeralda. Small wonder that the Legion considered Algeria their country, summed up in the statement that, 'Once a man has passed through one of the recruiting centres, all his future revolved around the African bases, irrespective of other postings, and to the headquarters at Sidi-bel-Abbès.'

Meanwhile the 2nd RE was fighting in the Aurès mountains. Savage fighting on 15 March 1844, overcame the fierce resistance of the Berber tribesmen defending their village of M'Chounech, earned the 2nd RE a regimental colour. The French were still being troubled by Abd-el-Kader (despite the success of the flying columns), who adopted the tactic of attacking from bases in Morocco, and in 1844 the angry Governor-General sent his forces across the border to occupy the town of Oujda. That they were forced by the politicians in Paris to withdraw was a move interpreted as weakness by Abd-el-Kader, who massed 40,000 men on the Algerian border, but he was defeated in a night attack on 13 August by 8,000 French troops, who included the 1st RE, whom Bugeaud had forced-marched to the battlefield at Oued Isly. As a result of this victory, Bugeaud received a dukedom, and the Sultan of Morocco had no option other than to sign the Treaty of Tangier, which provided for the internment of Abd-el-Kader if he again sought refuge in Moroccan territory. In the end he was captured and exiled, in December 1847, after which the area became reasonably peaceful, although in the intervening years the 1st RE had been involved in several hard fights with his followers. By a strange twist of fate, nearly a century later Abd-el-Kader's great-grandson joined the Legion, first fighting in Indo-China and later against the FLN (*Front de Libération Nationale*) in Algeria.

A period of relative calm occurred after the victory at M'Chounech but the Chauia tribesmen remained troublesome and, besides endeavouring to contain them, the 2nd RE commanded by Colonel Carbuccia was ordered, in July 1849, to attack a group of dissidents entrenched at the oasis of Zaatcha, near Biskra. Inadequately briefed and surprised by the strength of defences, the Legion's attack failed with the loss of thirty-two dead and 115 wounded. The French then withdrew and organized a second assault backed up by artillery and reinforcements, many recently arrived from France, who, suffering from cholera, brought the disease into the camp. Heavy artillery, commanded by General Herbillon, was necessary to force an entry into the oasis of Zaatcha, a huge palm grove surrounded by a ditch twenty feet (6 metres) wide protecting solid, inter-connecting buildings, occupied by experienced and determined defenders who had been told by their leader, Bou-Zian, that 'No infidel will ever pollute Zaatcha.' After the initial artillery barrage and in atrocious winter weather, the first assault, of 20 October, was repulsed, to be followed by another on 26 October. Captured or wounded men were tortured by the Berber women, who emasculated, blinded and beheaded their victims in full view of their comrades. The fighting was to last for six weeks before Zaatcha was taken on 26 November 1849. The legionnaires, like their enemies, gave no quarter. After the battle a spy pointed out Bou-Zian's house, which was blown open by legionnaires.into whose midst stepped a green-burnoosed figure with blue eyes and a wispy black beard. His hand clutched a Koran. 'I am Bou-Zian.' Later that morning Colonel Carbuccia was awakened to be shown, on three poles, the heads of Bou-Zian, his son and his religious teacher. The Zaatcha revolt was over but the action had cost Herbillon's force some 1,500 dead and wounded.

With Algeria more or less quiet except for some scattered areas, the new Emperor of the French, Napoleon III, agreed to join Britain in responding to the Turkish Government's call for support after Tsar Nicholas I of Russia had seized Constantinople in 1853. An 'Army of the Orient' was created, and in May 1854 an Imperial Ordinance transferred to it both the 1st and 2nd REs (except for a battalion of the 1st RE which remained in Algeria), renamed the 'Foreign Brigade'. After landing in the Crimea in October 1854, the 1st RE first saw action on 5 November, when it successfully repulsed a Russian attack at the cost of some 160 casualties.

After a first victory over the Russians at the Alma, the allies set out to besiege Sebastopol, with the result that the troops spent a dreadful winter without proper food, clothing or the provision of adequate shelter.

On 1 May 1855 the allies launched an offensive which failed, resulting in a massacre in which the Legion lost 480 wounded and 118 dead, among them Colonel Viénot of the 1st RE, who died at the head of his legionnaires. His name has been commemorated ever since as that of the Legion's barracks, first at Sidi-bel-Abbès, now at Aubagne. The failure of this attack led to a short lull, but on 18 June the Russians repulsed another attack by the allies, who suffered 6,000 casualties. On 8 September the Legion spearheaded a third assault, the one hundred volunteers carrying scaling-ladders and wooden beams with which they built scaffolding and ramps that enabled the main assault troops to overcome the defences. By evening the Malakoff (one of the two forts defending Sebastopol – the other was the Redan) had fallen, causing the Russians to start evacuating Sebastopol. On 10 September General Bazaine, veteran of Macta and the bloodbath at Barbastro, was named Commandant of the city of Sebastopol, which was then occupied by the Legion's Foreign Brigade.

There was scrounging for food and clothing, and two legionnaires poisoned the regimental mascot of the 23rd Royal Welsh Fusiliers, a magnificent billygoat named Dai. Following a solemn funeral at Inkerman cemetery, the coffin was dug up by the legionnaires, who skinned the animal and passed the fleece to a tanner and tailor, who turned it into a warm coat. Approached by a major from the Fusiliers, the legionnaire wearing it expected to be called forth to account for his actions but, after a brief conversation, was pleased to accept £20 for the coat!

Following an armistice, the Foreign Brigade disembarked at Oran on 6 July 1856, to the strains of a new march. (Not until 1870 did someone write down a parody of it and gave it the title '*Le Boudin*', 'The Black Pudding'.) After marching home to Sidi-bel-Abbès they received the unpleasant news that Napoleon III had announced in January 1855 the foundation of the 'Second Foreign Legion' to be composed entirely of Swiss personnel, who would wear a green uniform instead of the traditional blue. Returning veterans of Swiss nationality were immediately transferred to the Second Legion, but it was its redesignation as the 1st RE and the Crimean veterans as the 2nd RE which was considered insulting. The Crimean veterans could not easily accept that men they believed junior to themselves should be accorded the distinction of becoming the 1st RE.

However, there was no time for inter-regimental disputes because the completion of the pacification of Algeria required the subduing of the tribes in the rugged, snow-covered mountains of the Kabylia, a terrain which had even thwarted attempts at conquest by the troops of the Romans. Since 1838 the French had made a number of forays into these mountains – perhaps they were 'half-hearted' because of problems elsewhere; with these solved, it was decided to mount a major campaign. In 1856, over a period of eight months, a number of French columns (which included one battalion of the 1st RE and two of the 2nd RE who had marched out of Sidi-bel-Abbès to the strains of '*Le Boudin*') slowly converged on the rocky heart of Kabylia, fighting as they advanced to clear one ridge and valley after another until in June 1857 they arrived in front of the final obstacle – Ischeriden.

The ridge was held by between 4,000 and 5,000 tribesmen and, despite artillery support, the first French assault by two regiments of line infantry failed. General MacMahon, commanding the column ordered the 2nd RE into the attack. The bugle notes of '*Le Boudin*' sounded – '*En avant!*' – 'Advance!' – Major Paul Mangrin commanding the 2nd RE put his horse to the steep slope, the legionnaires following with arms shouldered as if on parade, not firing a shot – to the surprise of the Kabyle tribesmen. Veterans, the legionnaires knew that, if they halted and fired, they would never reload. Despite the hail of fire, they continued to advance, firing in unison only as they reached the cover and then fixing bayonets to complete their assault, which cleared the enemy from their defences in less than half an hour, so that the Legion added Ischeriden to its battle honours.

The political intrigues of Napoleon III resulted in the Legion's being ordered to Italy in support of that country's patriots, the Carbonari, who were struggling against the Austrian occupation of a large part of the country. During April 1859 the 1st RE was transferred to Bastia in Corsica to set up a depot and train new recruits, whilst the 2nd RE was re-organized into four battalions, one of which remained at Sidi-bel-Abbès whilst the other three, consisting of sixty officers and 1,400 NCOs and legionnaires, sailed for Marseilles. By May the regiments had been reunited in Genoa, where they joined the 2nd Zouaves to form Castagny's 2nd Brigade of Epinasse's 2nd Division of General MacMahon's 2nd Corps.

Tactical experience and training in Africa did not fit the Legion for its role in Italy, where the European armies of the day had evolved different techniques. However, on 4 June the French met the Austrian Army in front of the town of Magenta and, joining battle, the legionnaires found themselves at about 15.00 hours in thickly cultivated country ideal for infantry. As the white-coated Austrians advanced upon them, the horsemen of the French Mounted Riflemen started to fall back, but Colonel Granet Lacroix de Chabrière of the Legion stood up in his stirrups and ordered 'Packs off! – Forward the Legion!' Holding their bayonets low, the legionnaires charged forward, knocking the surprised Austrians off balance causing them to flee from the battlefield and giving victory to the French and to the Legion in particular. Sheer courage and physical effort had won the day, but in doing so fifteen Legion officers were dead or wounded, including Colonel de Chabrière (who died on 29 June 1859), together with 300 NCOs and legionnaires.

To celebrate the victory, legionnaires ran wild in the quiet market town, pillaging, looting and drinking to such an extent that not only were some found the next morning floating dead in the wine vats but, when Colonel José Martinez, commanding the 3rd Battalion, fearing an Austrian counter-attack, had '*Le Boudin*' sounded, Lieutenant Zede told him, 'The troops were too busy looting the wine cellars to bother with bugle calls!'

On the following day Milan was liberated, the Legion having earned the honour of marching into the city at the head of the French army. There the two regiments divided, the 1st RE to endeavour to recruit itself up to strength and the 2nd RE to join in the pursuit of the fleeing Austrians, whom they caught up with and defeated on 24 June, in a vicious struggle at Solferino. It was, however, a hollow victory, and Napoleon III quickly signed an armistice on 7 July 1859. Neither side had won and, for the cost of

12,000 French dead and wounded, 5,000 Italians and 13,000 Austrians, the struggle had merely nudged the Austrians out of one province. For home propaganda, the 'victorious' Army of Italy paraded through Paris on 14 August, and the legionnaires of the 2nd RE marched with them.

Returning to Algeria, the 2nd RE disembarked at Mers-el-Kebir on 22 August, marching back to Sidi-bel-Abbès. The 1st RE had returned direct to Bastia in Corsica on 7 August, where they remained until arriving back in Algeria during February 1860. Four months previously, on 14 October 1859, due to lack of recruits, the exclusive establishment by Swiss nationals of the 1st RE was abandoned and they reverted to wearing the blue tunics. However, from then onwards red and green became the colours of the Legion. Finally, in 1862, the 1st and 2nd REs once more joined together to form a single Foreign Regiment.

Within thirty years the Legion had evolved from a disorderly rabble to a brave and skilful fighting force which it was an honour to command, and traditions and customs had already evolved. Gradually it had begun to develop its own rules and, with its slow march, singing and motto '*Legio Patria Nostra*', created for itself an image of romanticism and heroism. Slowness of communications led the senior officers in Africa to act independently of French central authority – often out of necessity to cope with a particular situation. This independence of action also contributed to the Legion's individuality, and those who served with it had indeed found a homeland and become part of a family, harsh as it certainly was from time to time.

But the action which was to give the Legion its greatest strength of purpose, and which has been commemorated annually ever since, was yet to be fought.

3 Mexico, North Africa and the Great War

'Pero no son hombres, son demonios' –
'But they're devils, not men'
Colonel Combras to his Mexican troops at
the end of the battle of Camerone

The Legion found its tasks of construction and tax collection humdrum in comparison with active service and deeply resented their exclusion from the Mexican campaign, the latest adventure of Napoleon III which had arisen out of his support for the conservatives defeated in the most recent Mexican civil war. Cancellation by Mexico of its foreign debts led to France, Britain and Spain mounting an international expedition to Vera Cruz in January 1862, but after a short while only France remained, with Napoleon III reinforcing his garrison, having chosen the unemployed Austrian Archduke Maximilian to be Emperor.

Pressure by junior officers of the Legion on Napoleon III direct resulted in a *régiment de marche*,* consisting of 2,000 officers and men, formed into two seven-company battalions and a headquarters company, sailing from Mers-el-Kebir on 10 February, disembarking at Vera Cruz on 28 March 1863. What a reception! Disease was rampant and not only were the Legion to be excluded from the siege of Puebla but it was their thankless duty to guard part of the coast from the far edge of the low-lying 'hot lands', where cholera and yellow fever raged unchecked, to Chiquihuite where the headquarters was established. Service in this inhospitable land cost the Legion 800 dead with fever before the end of 1863.

Juarez, leader of the revolutionary Mexicans, and his 'freedom

* Experienced legionnaires assembled for a special task ('marching regiment').

fighters' were cruel and merciless killers who delighted in attacking and massacring the workers and guards of the isolated work camps along the route of the planned railway between the coast and Puebla. One such attack occurred on 18 April, the guerrillas being under the command of Antonio Diaz, Mayor of Jalapa; two days later, thinking to repeat his success, he came up against a company of the Legion, who cut their assailants to pieces, Lieutenant Milson killing Diaz with his own hand.

On 29 April Colonel Jeanningros, commanding the Legion, was informed that an important convoy consisting of 3 million francs worth of gold, rations and ammunition, together with vital equipment for use at the siege of Puebla, would be in transit over the insecure route from the coast. Aware of the effectiveness of the Juarist intelligence, Colonel Jeanningros decided to improve security by sending the third (duty) company down the road to meet and return with the convoy. Due to sickness, the company was reduced to sixty-two men without an officer, so Captain Danjou, the battalion adjutant, volunteered to take command, and he was accompanied by the paymaster, Second Lieutenant Vilain, and the standard-bearer, Second Lieutenant Maudet. The scene was set for an epic battle which has been singled out ever since as the most important day in the Legion's year.

On 30 April the third company was attacked by a force of 2,000 Mexicans at Camerone (an abandoned hamlet with a ruined mud-and-brick farmhouse). The valour of the legionnaires was such that they held out for eleven hours, inflicting at least 300 casualties on the Mexicans before the company was virtually wiped out. In the course of the action the convoy was saved, but it was the incredible act of courage when the five legionnaires still standing, without ammunition, fixed bayonets and charged the swarming Mexicans, that gave this defence its extraordinary significance in the annals of the Legion.* The battle has been remembered annually on 30 April ever since. First there is a parade, when the history of the battle is read out to all legionnaires; afterwards bonfires are lit and there are celebrations, when the old marching songs are sung. Such is the inspiration given by the sacrifice at Camerone that retreat is not considered by legionnaires, who have been renowned throughout their history for valour in the face of

* See Appendix 1 for a full account.

numerically superior forces. It is unfortunate that the example shown by Colonel Jeanningros when he received the news was so lacking, but it was at his request that Napoleon III decreed that the name of Camerone should be inscribed on the regimental colour.

Following the defence of Camerone, Mexican troops were still presenting arms at the spot a hundred years after the event. Before leaving Mexico, the Legion erected a small monument at the site, and in 1892, with Mexican co-operation, this was replaced by a monument bearing an inscription that sums up not only the battle but the spirit of the legionnaire: 'Here stood fewer than sixty men against an entire army. Its weight overwhelmed them. Life, sooner than courage, forsook these soldiers of France.' Of these some twenty legionnaires survived the battle, although many of them subsequently died from the wounds they received.

Captain Danjou had been wounded in the Crimea and wore a wooden artificial left hand which was found on the battlefield. It is a sacred relic of the Legion and at Aubagne is paraded before the legionnaires on the day of the Fête de Camerone.

Camerone did not end the Legion's presence in Mexico, and it was not until the Prussian army, utilizing rail transport for movement and breech-loading rifles to such an effect that they destroyed the Austrian army at Sadowa in July 1866, brought potential trouble for Napoleon III that he rescinded his order to the Legion to support the 'puppet' Maximilian for as long as possible. As a result the last legionnaire sailed from Vera Cruz on 27 February 1867, for Algeria. Maximilian, ignoring all suggestions to flee, was executed by firing squad some three months later at Queretaro.

Perhaps it was the aftermath of Mexico, or the routine of construction with only occasional skirmishes involving dissident tribesmen, but morale in the Legion was low, and when the Franco-Prussian war broke out in July 1870, it was foreigners resident in France who came forward to fight for their adopted homeland. Hastily recruited into a fifth Foreign Battalion nominally part of the Legion, these enthusiastic volunteers were nearly wiped out before Orleans on 10 October 1870, the survivors being incorporated into two battalions of the Legion which had arrived from Algeria at Toulon the next day. (This step contravened the original ordinance of 1831 which specifically excluded legionnaires from combat in mainland France.) They fought bitterly through a hard winter, losing fourteen officers, fifty-two NCOs and 864 legionnaires, before the Armistice was signed on 28 January 1871. However, before they could return to Algeria, the Paris Commune broke out in open rebellion, and so legionnaires fought Frenchmen on the streets of Paris before order was restored, allowing them to leave the capital on 11 June, arriving back in Algeria on the 22nd. The defeat of France encouraged many of the tribes to 'take on the French', but a number of short, sharp actions soon disabused them of their new-found confidence to such an extent that by 1871 relative peace had been established in the pacified areas.

For the Legion, its confirmed establishment in July 1871 being five eight-company battalions, it was a period of consolidation. Recruiting was satisfactory, and in 1875 the official title reverted to '*Légion Etrangère*'.

There were no great campaigns to disrupt the monotonous patrolling and construction but political events were moving in a direction that would considerably affect the Legion in the closing years of the nineteenth century. During 1881 a series of vicious battles took place with Arab tribesmen, led by an able chief named Bou-Amama. Also during this period Colonel de Négrier became the commanding officer of the Legion, from 7 July, 1881. After a period of relative peace, he came at the right time, invigorating and re-organizing the legionnaires, including the formation of a new type of unit, a company issued with mules and designated 'mounted company'. In essence the arrangement was that two men were allocated to each mule, one riding and the other marching – often at the double – for periods of up to one hour. Only a minimum of kit was carried on the mule and none by the legionnaire. Only experienced and particularly fit men were recruited for this 'elite within an elite', which achieved a number of spectacular successes against the warring, nomadic Arab tribes. Another important development, which occurred in October 1881, authorized the open enlistment of French nationals into the Legion.

It was from this point that expansion of the Legion and French colonial policy resulted in contingents of legionnaires being posted to a number of overseas theatres besides increasing activity in Algeria against rebel tribesmen. In April 1882 the 1st Mounted Company became involved in a famous action in a valley known as Chotti Tigri, near Naci-bel-Salem. On this occasion some 250 legionnaires, accompanied by a troop of cavalry, were escorting a group of cartographers engaged in a major survey of the area when they were attacked by at least 2,500 tribesmen, of whom 1,000 were mounted. It was a vicious battle, much of it being fought hand to hand, and it cost the Legion fifty-one dead and twenty-eight wounded. The relief column was led by Colonel de Négrier, who found that many of the Legion's dead had been dug up and severely mutilated.

At this time the attention of the French 19th Army Corps was turning more towards Morocco, which was very much a refuge of the tribesmen who attacked a Saharan relief column of 3,000 pack camels on 2 September 1903. It was a battle which has been compared to Camerone and which involved a half company of the 22nd (Mounted) Company of the 2nd RE, which consisted of two officers, 113 legionnaires and thirty Spahi troopers under the command of Captain Vauchez. Attacked mid-morning at El Moungar by some 2,000 warriors loyal to Bou-Amama, the legionnaires fought amongst the rocks without water or rations and, towards the end, with very little ammunition, until at about 17.30 a relief mounted company of the 1st RE arrived at the double. Captain Vauchez died of his wounds and was buried on the battlefield with Lieutenant Selchauhansen and thirty-five legionnaires. A further forty-seven were wounded.

Such incidents led the French to decide to clean up the area once and for all, and Colonel Lyautey, recently arrived from Tonkin, was given the task. It was here that the policy was developed whereby the country was divided up into sectors, securing each with a number of military posts in the heart of a delicate area or suspect village, making the area insecure to the enemy by frequent patrolling, thereby establishing the French presence and hopefully reassuring the population so that they would support the French. It took until 1934 to accomplish the task, largely by the tireless efforts of the three mounted companies, which often covered forty miles in a day to make great use of surprise and unpredictability in their attacks.

France took it upon itself to establish a 'protectorate' in Morocco, which was not considered 'part of France' as was Algeria, and though nominal power was vested in a succession of Sultans, various pretexts were used to establish a military presence. When, in 1911, the capital, Fez, was occupied by the French, the 3rd (Mounted) Company of the 1st Battalion of the 2nd RE was under the command of Captain Rollet, later to be so identified with the Legion that he was known as 'the Father of the Foreign Legion'. In March 1912 the Treaty of Fez legalized the French 'protectorate' over Morocco, and General Lyautey returned from a corps command in France to be Resident-General in Morocco. To consolidate their presence, the French constructed numerous forts, blockhouses and connecting roads – tasks in which the Legion was closely involved, besides continuing to pacify the country, which resulted in almost continuous fighting with dissident tribesmen who rose again in revolt whilst France was heavily engaged in World War I.

In September 1883 Colonel de Négrier was promoted to general and left the Legion to command an expeditionary force to Indo-China. One of his first actions was to call for a volunteer battalion of legionnaires to serve in Tonkin. It landed at Haiphong on 8 November 1883, to be greeted by General de Négrier's famous address: 'You legionnaires are soldiers in order to die, and I am sending you where you can die.' With Major Dominé in command, the 600 legionnaires joined 5,000 marines and infantry under Admiral Courbet at Hanoi. Tonkin was the northernmost province of the Empire of Annam, whose Emperor requested the French to assist in combatting the large bands of pirates (known as 'black flags') who largely controlled the province.

Admiral Courbet decided, in 1883, to clear out the Chinese and the brigands they supported who occupied two main centres, at Son Tay and Bac Ninh. On 16 December, as part of a force of 5,000, French troops took part in the assault on the Son Tay stockaded fortress held by 20,000 Chinese. The attack faltered and de Négrier sent in the Legion, but even they had difficulty in penetrating the defence until a Corporal Minnaert, a giant Belgian sapper, came forward and, wielding his axe, leapt across the moat, forcing his way through a gap blown in the stockade, to seize a black standard, shouting, 'Long live Belgium! Long live the Legion!' This so astonished the Chinese that their momentary lapse in concentration cost them the battle as they were scattered by legionnaires at the point of the bayonet. Later, as Admiral Courbet pinned the Military Medal on Minnaert's chest, he told him, 'Had you waved the Tricolor and cried *"Vive la France!"*, I would have given you the Legion of Honour".

On 24 February 1884, reinforced by the recently arrived 2nd Battalion, the Legion took part in the successful storming of the citadel of Bac Ninh. General de Négrier who led this action declared afterwards that, 'The honour of being the first into Bac Ninh belongs to the Legion.'

After the battle, the two battalions parted, and the first supported by gunboats captured the 'black flag' fort at Tuyen Quang, leaving the 3rd and 4th Companies (later relieved by the 1st and 2nd Companies) as the backbone of a 600-strong garrison. Early in January, the fort was cut off by a force of well-trained and well-armed 'black flags' supported by Chinese regular troops, who besieged the garrison for almost two months. At the outset of the action, the enemy surrounded Tuyen Quang with a belt of trenches from which they mounted their infantry attacks, supported by frequent artillery bombardments. By 11 February, the Chinese sappers had blown up the south-east corner of the walls, which was followed by fierce hand-to-hand fighting, and this pattern was to continue for the rest of February, resulting in the walls being breached in six places, which were then barricaded by the defenders against enemy attacks. Matters were becoming desperate, but an Annamite coolie who had been sent out with a request for help returned on 26 February with the simple message – 'The relief column is on its way.' This gave the defenders renewed energy, so much so that Captain de Borelli's legion company captured two black flags from the Chinese, which he bequeathed to the Legion on condition that they were never taken to France, such was his bitterness at the treatment he subsequently received from the French Government.

When the relief column arrived, on 3 March 1885, the defenders presented arms to their rescuers, a gesture which was to become a tradition in Indo-China.

This epic defence cost the Legion thirty-two dead and 126 wounded, which involved all six officers, in addition to a company commander who was killed. Captain de Borelli later wrote a poem 'To My Dead', which remains one of the most famous tributes to the legionnaire. It is dedicated to one Thiebald Steibler who gave his life to save his officer during a sortie in the last night of the siege. Some of the lines from this poem of twenty-seven verses are as follows:

A mes hommes qui sont morts,
Mes compagnons, c'est moi; mes hommes gens de guerre,
C'est votre chef d'hier qui vient parler ici
De ce qu'on ne sait pas, ou que l'on ne sait guère;
Mes morts, je vous salue, et je vous dis: Merci.

Il serait temps qu'en France on se prit de vergogne
A connaître au si mal la vieille Légion
De qui, pour l'avoir vu à sa dure besogne
J'ai très grande amour et la religion.

Or, écoutez ceci: Déserteurs! mercenaires!
Ramassis d'étrangers sans honneur et sans foi!
C'est de vous qu'il s'agit; de vous Légionnaires!
Ayez-en le coeur net, et demandez pourquoi?

Sans honneur? Ah! passons! – Et sans foi? Qu'est ce à dire?
Que fallait-il de plus et qu'aurait-on voulu?
N'avez vous pas tenu, tenu jusqu'au martyre
La parole donnée et la marche conclue?

Dormez dans la grandeur de votre sacrifice,
Dormez, que nul regret ne vous vienne hanter;
Dormez dans cette paix large et libératrice
Où ma penace en deuil ira vous visiter!

Je sais où retrouver, à leur suprème étape,
Tous ceux dont la grande herbe a bu le sang vermeil
Et ceux qu'ont engloutis les pièges de la sape
Et ceux qu'ont dévorés la fièvre et le soleil.

To my men who are dead,
My companions – it is I; my good warriors,
It's your leader who is talking to you here
Of what one does not know, or hardly knows;
My dead men, I salute you, and I say to you: Thank you.

It would be time to be ashamed in France
To accord evil to the old Legion,
For which, having seen it in desperate need,
I have such great love and reverence.

But listen! Deserters! Mercenaries!
Full of foreigners without honour or faith!
It's because of you that it is ashamed: of you legionnaires!
Be honest with yourselves and ask why.

Without honour? Let it go. And without faith? Who's to say?
Should they do more? what do you want of them?
Haven't you kept faith, even to martyrdom,
Your word kept, the march finished?

Sleep in the grandeur of your sacrifice,
Sleep and let no regret haunt you;
Sleep in that great freedom-giving peace
Where my mourning spirit will visit you!

I know where to find, at their last halt,
All whose red blood was drunk by the green grass,
And those who were engulfed by mine-traps
And who were eaten up by fever and the sun.

At about the same time, the 2nd Battalion of the 1st RE and the 2nd Battalion of the 2nd RE were taking part in General de Négrier's 2nd Brigade's action in the area of Lang San. From a military point of view, this struggle was somewhat inconclusive, despite heavy fighting and a French withdrawal where the Legion formed the rearguard. However, it was sufficient to bring about an armistice, on 1 April 1885, between the French and the Chinese. This did not immediately stop all the fighting, and the Legion was much involved in fighting with inter-warring bands of brigands and tribesmen. On 21 January 1885 the 4th Battalion of the 2nd RE disembarked at Kelung in Formosa to take part in an action against the Chinese, who were occupying the high ground, and between 4 and 7 March the legionnaires successfully dislodged the Chinese from their fortified position on the Charbon mountain. They pressed home their attack to the River Tam-Sui and on their camps at Loüan-Louan. Operations ceased on 17 March, and the 4th returned to Indo-China, patrolling the frontier of Annam from their base at Phu Nho Quang. The Legion's ability and experience in policing, construction and organization gradually brought about a peaceful society which caused Tonkin to be a popular posting for legionnaires. Demands for manpower reduced the garrison until by 1917 only one battalion remained; in 1919 this too was withdrawn. The first unit to return – in 1920 – was the 4th Battalion of the 1st RE. Various re-organizations then took place, until on 1 September 1930 the 5th Foreign Infantry Regiment (5th REI) was formed from the four battalions of the 1st REI operating in Indo-China.

France had established several small trading-posts along the coast of Africa, and until 1892 no problems had arisen insofar as their safety was guaranteed by a treaty of friendship with the local king, Behanzin. However, since the Franco-Prussian war of 1870, German agents had been spreading rumours to the effect that France no longer existed and that it was time to be rid of the French presence. Their persuasive propaganda was complemented by the supply of new Mauser rifles and German instructors to train the recipients in their use. With his new-found confidence, Behanzin started to harass the French posts, in particular Ouidah, a small port on the coast of Dahomey currently known as Benin. To put an end to this problem, an expedition of 4,000 French troops, commanded by Colonel Dodds, which included *a bataillon de marche* of the Legion under Major Faroux, disembarked at Cotonou on 26 August 1892.

The column moved off northwards in the direction of Behanzin's capital, Abomey, a distance of about sixty-five miles (104 kilometres). Progress was slow but without serious incident as the troops hacked their way with machetes through the dense undergrowth, until on 11 September they met up at the Oueme river with a detachment sent on ahead to pacify the Déçamé area. Together the united forces followed the course of the river until they reached Dogba on 18 September. It was here, where they bivouacked amongst the trees, with the river on one side and the camp entrenched on the other three, that Behanzin's warriors attacked. After the initial shock the Legion mounted a counter-attack with the bayonet – their traditional response to such a situation – but on this occasion it cost the life of Major Faroux, whose last words to Colonel Dodds asked the question, 'Were you satisfied with my men?' This bloody battle lasted two hours and cost the Legion forty-five dead and sixty wounded. Behanzin lost 800 dead, amongst them many women warriors who fought to the death rather than be taken prisoner.

The long, slow march continued, with many ambushes, and scarcity of food and water, and it was not until 17 November that the column reached Abomey, to find the town in flames and Behanzin gone, although he was captured some months later. Four hundred and fifty legionnaires had escaped death, wounds and disease, and when they returned to Algeria in February 1894 they took back with them as a trophy a white parasol, edged with fifty human lower jaws, as a grim reminder of Behanzin's taste for human sacrifice.

Slavery was a problem which plagued the French authorities through north-west Africa, and in support of the Government's efforts to stamp it out, 120 legionnaires and four officers of the 2nd RE arrived in September 1892 at Kayes on the Senegal river, where they were issued with mules and formed a mounted company.

The most important Legion operations in French Sudan took place in the region of Kayes and at Timbuktu. At the fortified village of Bosse, some ninety legionnaires with 200 Senegalese took on over a thousand enemy and after their Commander, Lieutenant Betbeder was seriously wounded, the assault was led by Sergeant Minnaert, himself wounded, who had already earned a great reputation at the taking of Son Tay ten years previously.

French honour and interests were at stake in their protectorate of Madagascar due to Queen Ranavolo III's failing to honour the treaty with France of 1885, and on 23 April 1895 a force of 21,600 under the command of General Duchêne, which included one battalion of the Legion, 7,000 porters and several hundred vehicles, arrived in Madagascar to reassert French influence. There was no road between the landing point and the capital, Tananarive, a distance of 250 miles (402 kilometres), with the result that the troops had to build one. Such were the conditions of extreme heat and disease that 5,756 men died – seven in battle, thirteen from wounds and the remainder of heatstroke and disease.

With the Legion always as the spearhead and inspiration for the remainder, they led a forced march of the 4,000 fittest men for the last 125 miles (201 kilometres) reaching the capital on 30 September. On the following day General Duchêne addressed the legionnaires: 'It is thanks to you, gentlemen, that we are here at all. If ever I have the honour to command another expedition, I shall ask for at least a battalion of the Foreign Legion.'

Although this battalion returned to Algeria in December, a new *bataillon de marche* was formed from both foreign regiments, landing in Madagascar in August 1896, where it remained until 1904 as part of the occupation force of General Gallieni. They were joined by further detachments – in particular, in March 1900, the 4th Battalion of the 1st RE and the 2nd Battalion of the 2nd RE, who were recalled in April 1901 and November 1903 respectively.

The 'war to end all wars' – World War I – started on 1 August 1914, when Germany declared war on Russia. On the same day the French Army mobilized. On 3 August the British Expeditionary force did likewise, and Germany declared war on France, repeating the events of 1870 when many foreign nationals living in and out of France volunteered for the army and were assembled in camps around Paris. It was decided to place them in two new *régiments de marche* of the Legion, established at Mailly Camp in September 1914 (the 2nd Marching Regiment of the 1st RE and the 2nd Marching Regiment of the 2nd RE), each with four battalions with the cadre of each made up of veteran legionnaires from Morocco and Algeria.

Another *régiment de marche*, the 3rd Marching Regiment of the 1st RE, was then formed in the Paris area and, besides foreign volunteers, included drafts from the police and fire brigade. It was disbanded in March 1915, most of its volunteers being transferred to their own national armies and the remainder to the 2nd Marching Regiment of the 1st RE. Finally a regiment consisting entirely of Italians came into existence in November 1914 and was given the designation 4th Marching Regiment of the 1st RE. It was, in fact, the first regiment to see action when it took part, on Christmas Eve, in an unsuccessful attack in Bolante Woods on the Argonne, followed by another, this time successful, attack two days later at Courtes-Chausses. Both of these actions were costly in dead and wounded, and the regiment was further weakened during heavy fighting in January 1915. When Italy entered the war, her Government requested the repatriation of the survivors, who were assimilated into the Italian Army.

In May 1915 the 2nd Marching Regiment of the 1st RE suffered heavy casualties when it took part in the Battle of Artois, and although it took its objective, the so-called 'White Works' on Hill 140, its losses were such that the regiment was forced to withdraw in the face of an enemy counter-attack. It was, in fact, the Queen's Own Regiment, formed of Bermondsey men, which went to the rescue of the Legion. Subsequently the Queen's re-took Hill 140 – but at the cost of a whole battalion. Despite its reduced strength, the regiment was again in action on 15/16 June before Givenchy, the two assaults costing some 2,700 legionnaires dead, wounded or missing.

Meanwhile the 2nd Marching Regiment of the 2nd RE had seen action in the Rheims and Paissy sectors before joining with the 2nd Marching Regiment of the 1st RE in September 1915, at the battle of Navarin Farm in Champagne, east of Berry-au-Bac. Just before the bugle sounded the charge, Captain Junot, a veteran of the Legion now wearing his full dress uniform, mounted the parapet above the trenches and shouted to his men, 'My children, we are going to certain death, but we are going to try to die like brave men.'

Amongst those who fought at Navarin Farm was a British legionnaire, John Ford Elkington. He was decorated for his bravery, the citation reading 'The Military Medal and Croix de Guerre are conferred upon John Ford Elkington, Legionnaire in Company B3 of the First Foreign Regiment.' Although fifty years old, he had given proof during the campaign of remarkable courage and ardour, setting everyone the best example. 'He was gravely wounded on 28 September 1915, rushing forward to assault enemy trenches. He has lost the use of his right leg.' J.F. Elkington was the first to receive the immediate award of the newly created Croix de Guerre, three months after its inception. A professional soldier in the British Army, he had been court-martialled and cashiered for alleged cowardice after his battalion had been severely mauled at Mons. Exhausted and hungry, he had agreed, for the sake of his men, to sign a document for the Mayor of St-Quentin before the latter would agree to help his ally, agreeing to surrender his men to the Germans if they advanced on the town. As it happened, the Germans did not attack St-Quentin, but Elkington was not to be spared and was dismissed from the service for conduct that 'rendered him unfit and incapable of serving his Sovereign in the future in any military capacity', whereupon he joined the Legion.

With the award, Elkington lost his anonymity, and the citation was read by King George V, who requested that the following notice appear in the *London Gazette*: 'The King has been graciously pleased to approve the re-instatement of John Ford Elkington in the rank of Lieutenant-Colonel of the Royal Warwickshire Regiment, with his previous seniority, in consequence of his gallant conduct whilst serving in the ranks of the Foreign Legion of the French Army.' The King also awarded Elkington the DSO.

So horrific was the action at Navarin Farm that afterwards the regiments were disbanded, the survivors being remustered into the Foreign Legion Marching Regiment (RMLE), consisting of seventy-one officers and 3,115 NCOs and legionnaires in three battalions. Such was its fighting spirit that, in the three years between its formation on 11 November 1915 and the armistice on 11 November 1918, it was to become the most decorated unit in the French army.

A new commandant took over the battalion in which most of the Americans served, Colonel James Waddell, a New Zealander who had studied at a British university, and joined the British Army, which he had left at the age of twenty-seven to join the Legion in 1900, subsequently fighting in Tonkin and around Colomb-Bechar (Algeria). Seriously wounded whilst fighting in the Dardanelles, he had been awarded the Legion of Honour and the Croix de Guerre with seven palms.

The new regiment's first action took place between 4 and 9 July 1916, at Belloy-en-Santerre, as part of the French Somme offensive. It cost the regiment twenty-five officers and 844 men dead, including the American poet Alan Seeger, whose father was later to present a bell to the church at Belloy in memory of his son, who lies in an unknown grave. Among other Americans who served was Bob Scanlon, the Negro boxer, Hendrick van Loon, the distinguished historian, and two surgeons, Legionnaire Bywater, aged seventy-two, and Legionnaire Wilson, aged sixty-nine, both of whom were Seventh-Day Adventists who refused to fire their rifles, observing that they had not joined to fight against Germany but 'for the mud baths – the trenches are very healthy!'. Regrettably they died before they could prove this – or be disproved.

After involvement in preparations for the 1917 spring offensive in the area of the River Aisne, the RMLE's next major action commenced at dawn on 17 April with an attack on the edge of the village of Auberive in the Snippes Valley. It took three days and nights of bloody fighting from shell-hole to shell-hole, always in deep mud, to capture the German trench line, the pre-attack artillery barrage having failed to destroy the German machine-gun nests which inflicted heavy casualties on the attackers, including the death of the commandant, Lt.-Col. Duriez. It was an incredible success for the RMLE, which had captured $4\frac{1}{2}$ miles of German trenches in a war where success was measured in hundreds of yards. Sheer exhaustion resulted in the RMLE being withdrawn from the front line and sent to recuperate at Mailly, where they were joined by Lieutenant-Colonel Rollet, already a personality of the Legion who had made his name with the mounted companies in South Oran and Morocco. A small, dry man with a bristling beard, who always wore his old desert uniform, no shirt and boots without socks, he had the honour, on 14 July 1917, to lead an honour guard in Paris at a ceremony where the President of the Republic personally pinned to the colour of the RMLE the yellow-and-green lanyard of the Military Medal. It was in recognition not only of the regiment's combat achievements but also of their loyalty to France at a time when the reliability of the French Army was in doubt, elements in fifty-four divisions having been in open revolt in the aftermath of the disastrous campaign.

On 20/21 August under Rollet's leadership the RMLE achieved a notable victory at Cumières in the Verdun sector, securing all their objectives in less than the allotted time, taking 680 prisoners and fifteen guns at a cost of fifty-three dead and 271 wounded or missing. Any death is tragic, but this was considered minimal losses, taking into account that the wholesale slaughter of thousands had become the 'norm' on the Western Front. A contributing factor was an important change in the Legion's tactics: no more shell-fire parades lining up to be slaughtered by the traversing German machine-guns, but actions by sections of twelve men, who kept low, running, creeping or crawling from cover to cover as they progressed to their objectives.

On 27 September General Pétain reviewed the Legion, awarding them the Legion of Honour for their conduct at Verdun, which necessitated the invention of a crimson lanyard that was officially worn from 3 November 1917.

After a period in the Flirey sector, the Moroccan Division, which included the RMLE, was rushed to the Amiens sector to repel the German advance which had broken through the Allied lines on 21 March. After digging in, the legionnaires attacked on 25 April at Hangard Wood, where the Germans had annihilated several thousands of men by bombarding the woods with mustard gas. Although it was successful, they sustained appalling losses –

eighteen officers and 833 men. For a time the 1st Battalion of the RMLE was commanded by Legionnaire Kemmlet from Luxembourg, a wounded veteran who took command after all the officers had fallen in the first attack. After a short rest, the RMLE was committed to action on 29 May in the area of Soissons and despite a bloody battle were not dislodged from their positions, thereby preventing a German advance on Paris. In fact, in his memoirs, General von Ludendorff observed that this defence contributed to the failure of his offensive.

On 18 July 1918 the Allies went over to the offensive. It was a new experience, for the Legion was to go into action near St-Pierre-Aigle supported by Renault light tanks. As the legionnaires fought hand to hand with the Germans, machine-gun fire from the tanks kept their reinforcements at bay for the legionnaires to attack with the bayonet. In three days of fierce fighting, the Legion reached the Château Thierry/Soissons Wood area but lost 780 men, including Major Marseille and Captain de Sampigny, successive commanders of the 3rd Battalion.

The Legion's last battle of the war commenced on 2 September 1918 and lasted for thirteen days and nights of continuous fighting, during which the RMLE broke through the Hindenburg line in the area of Laffaux at Vauxaillon Tunnel. It was while they were resting that General Mangin ordered that the tunnel be taken, and to inspire his exhausted legionnaires Rollet marched at the head of his men, followed by a drummer and a few buglers playing '*Le Boudin*'. It was a murderous walk through the cutting, with fire from friend and foe cutting through their ranks. Few survived the walk through the tunnel; those who did cracked the Hindenburg line but it cost the Legion 1,433 officers and men – almost fifty per cent of its strength at the outset of the battle, in which the Germans again used poison gas.

Throughout World War I some 42,883 legionnaires served on the Western Front, of whom 36,644 were foreigners (280 British) and 6,239 French; 4,931 were known dead and 25,000 wounded or posted missing – many of them killed. The most highly decorated French soldier of the war was Legion Sergeant-Major Mader – a German.

After the armistice on 11 November 1918, the RMLE returned to Africa but it was not until 1 January 1921 that it was designated the 3rd REI, consisting of three battalions, based at Fez. Its regimental colours, decorated with the Military Medal and the Legion of Honour, nine times mentioned in despatches, were entrusted to the new regiment.

France was not the only theatre of war where the Legion saw service. The 1st African Marching Regiment (1st RMA), raised in February 1915 and consisting of Zouaves and legionnaires, went into action on 28 April 1915 in the Dardanelles. In the bitter fighting which followed, the 3rd Battalion, which consisted of legionnaires from the 1st and 2nd REs, was quickly reduced in strength, and it was not until the summer that reinforcements arrived in the shape of 700 veterans from Indo-China. The 1st RMA was then transferred to Salonika, where it fought the Bulgarians for nearly two years. Then, its strength reduced to 200 legionnaires, the survivors returned to Africa before being absorbed into the RMLE.

At the end of the war three rifle companies and a machine-gun company were raised locally in northern Russia, where they took part in the fierce fighting against the Bolsheviks during the Allied intervention. Following the fighting before Archangel, where the Red Army's advance was halted, the unit was disbanded, although many of the former legionnaires joined the White Russians and continued fighting in French uniforms in the defence of Petrograd under their local unit commanders. At the end of the fighting a number of the survivors made their way to Sidi-bel-Abbès where they re-enlisted in the Legion: *Legio Patria Nostra* – the Legion is our homeland indeed!

At the time of the formation of the RMLE and in accordance with the customs of the Legion, legionnaires who did not wish to fight against their own country were exempted from such involvement. As a result, the African garrisons continued consisting mostly of men with German, Austrian, Bulgarian and Turkish nationality. It was this much-depleted force which enabled Lyautey, the French Resident-General in Morocco to interpret liberally his orders from the French Government ('Hold on to useful Morocco') to continue with tasks he had originally agreed to undertake. Although some posts were abandoned, others were held under almost continuous siege by tribesmen aided and encouraged by German agents. Despite many actions, some involving fierce fighting, Lyautey managed to maintain his tenuous hold on Morocco, an inheritance which was preserved intact for the legionnaires returning to Africa at the end of World War I.

In the aftermath of the war, the Legion set about re-organization. Indeed, so impressive had been its achievements that the French Government even considered the creation of a complete brigade. This did not happen. On 5 August 1920 the French Government authorized the creation of the foreign cavalry, artillery and engineering units but in the end only the cavalry regiment was established, the 1st Foreign Cavalry Regiment (1st REC) formed in Tunisia on 8 March 1921, from elements of the 2nd REI. The new regiment contained officers and NCOs from French army cavalry regiments together with many former White Russian cavalrymen, who had become political exiles. Its establishment resulted in the other regiments having to include the designation 'Infantry' in their titles. There was no shortage of recruits for all the Legion regiments, with men from reduced or disbanded armies rubbing shoulders with those who for one reason or another had no acceptable home. As previously mentioned, the RMLE was re-formed as the 3rd REI, which was commanded by Colonel Rollet until 1926, when he took over command of the 1st REI, where he remained until 1931 when he became 'Inspector-General of the Legion'.

Throughout the twenties and thirties the Legion's efforts were concentrated in Morocco, with units generally operating in battalion strength and taking the name of their commander, i.e. *bataillon Goret* rather than the official number, which in this case was the 6th Battalion of the 1st REI. Besides restoring order, considerable constructional work was undertaken, including the famous tunnel at Foum-Zabal hewn out of solid rock for a distance of 200 feet to a height of ten feet and a width of twenty-five feet by the Sapper-Pioneer Company of the 3rd REI using only picks, shovels and crowbars. An inscription at the entrance to the tunnel records the event: 'The mountain barred our way. The order was given to pass nonetheless. The Legion carried it out.'

Heavy fighting took place on several occasions during the continued pacification of Morocco, and on 6 May 1923 the 3rd Battalion of the 3rd REI won a mention in despatches after a continuous battle lasting twelve hours against Ait Tserouchen warriors who outnumbered the battalion two to one. A new leader, Abd-el-Krim, managed to establish an army of 100,000 Berber tribesmen from the Riff Mountains and at Anoual in July 1921 annihilated 12,000 Spanish troops in their Moroccan coastal enclave. This action brought down the Spanish Government and encouraged Abd-el-Krim to believe he could beat the French, who allied with the Spanish. Some of Abd-el-Krim's forces were trained by a former German legionnaire, Joseph Klems, who deserted in 1922 after a broken love affair. After the Riff surrendered in 1926, he escaped into the Riff Mountains but, betrayed by the youngest of his four wives, surrendered, ill with fever, to a Legion section which had surrounded his hiding-place. He was sentenced to death at his court-martial, but this was commuted to life imprisonment on Devil's Island. However, as a result of world opinion (formed by Press reports which had turned him into a desert hero whose name was to be immortalized in Sigmund Romberg's operetta *The Desert Song*), he was released after seven years, returning to live in Berlin, where he died shortly before World War II, after slashing his wrists in a police cell following his arrest on suspicion of a minor crime.

After several bitter battles between the tribesmen and the French, in which no quarter was given by either side and cruelty became the order of the day, the decisive battles were fought by the 2nd REI at Djebel Iskritten and Targuist, bringing about Abd-el-Krim's surrender on 26 May 1926, although it was not until 24 March 1933 after much more fighting that the last rebel chief submitted.

A former British legionnaire recalling one such skirmish in which he took part, in company with a mounted company as part of a detachment sent to relieve a fort, tells how the legionnaires sighted the Riff tribesmen mounted on camels and horses and were ordered down into a defensive position. 'Load. Safety catches off. Don't fire until ordered,' shouted their sergeant. As he unholstered his revolver, he said, 'Have you seen one of these before? Now this is not for the enemy, it is for you. The first man who stands up when the Riffs charge will be shot for desertion. Now you know.' When the expected attack came, the Sergeant ordered, 'Don't aim for the riders, aim for the camels – you've more chance of hitting them.' So much for marksmanship. Following the order, 'Fire', the Sergeant shouted, 'No prisoners, none at all. If anyone moves, shoot to kill.' Fortunately, when the Riffs got within fifty yards of the legionnaires, they swerved and withdrew. Sensing victory, the legionnaires stood up and cheered, but their Sergeant told them, 'Don't get excited.

They'll be back, and I didn't tell you to stand up – down!' Just as the Riffs had regrouped, they sighted the returning mounted company who had gone ahead to the fort. The Riffs withdrew and, mission accomplished, the legionnaires turned around and marched back to camp.

The League of Nations made Syria a French mandated territory after World War I but after a period of relative peace, during which the French were establishing themselves, the Druze tribes of the Seynan hills rebelled, and on 22 July 1925 7,000 of them decimated a Legion company led by Captain Normand, the survivors taking refuge in an old fort at Soueida, which was then besieged. A relief column which included a platoon of armoured cars was attacked by 3,000 Druzes at the village of Messifré at 01.00 hours on 17 September 1925, the battle lasting until the afternoon. It involved hand-to-hand fighting during the night, and it was not until the following afternoon, when three French aircraft bombed the base and camel lines of the Druzes, who faltered in their attack, that they withdrew, enabling the road to Soueida to be re-opened.

In November a similar action was fought at Rachaya with even more savagery and again involving the use of aircraft to bomb the attacking Druzes. This time the situation had been even more desperate, and with ammunition down to fifteen rounds per man, the legionnaires had been preparing for a repetition of Camerone. These two battles were indeed a 'baptism of fire' for the 1st REC but their ability and courage brought about a justified claim that is immortalized in the regimental song:

> When a Foreign Legion column marched through, the Syrian bled.
> It is the 1st Foreign Cavalry that forms the column's head.

Things were never the same again for the Druzes and after a few skirmishes their rebellion died out, leaving the Legion to police and garrison Syria, where in October 1939 the four battalions were amalgamated into a new three-battalion regiment designated the 6th Foreign Infantry Regiment (6th REI); it remained in the country until 1941.

Perhaps part of the romance surrounding the Legion in the twenties and thirties may be attached to the flamboyant characters who served with it at this time. It was the time of the '*caids*', the great

A legionnaire in full campaign dress, North Africa, 1903–11

Colonel de Négrier

The first legionnaires, 18[

The wounded of Camerone, 1863

A colour party presenting the flag of the Foreign Legion at Sidi-bel-Abbès in 1906

Top left: Lieutenant-Colonel Rollet with the colour of the RMLE in 1918, flanked by four Chevaliers of the Legion of Honour from the regiment. Rollet's portrait is now displayed in all barracks used by the Legion. *Top right:* A cavalier of the 1st REC in Syria, 1924. *Below:* 1931 – celebrating 100 years of the Legion

Two Chinese legionnaires in Morocco, 1931, reading a letter from home

Legionnaires of the 13th DBLE with an FM 24/29 on the shore of a
Norwegian lake, 1940

James Williamson, who joined the Legion in 1937 as James Cavanagh and fought with the 13th DBLE in Norway

James Williamson's record of service

RECRUTEMENT LEGION ETRANGERE

Classe I 9 3 7

NUMÉRO L. M. 7I.I37

VIIᵉ RÉGION MILITAIRE

1ᵉʳ RÉGIMENT ÉTRANGER

Service 5° SECTION

ÉTAT SIGNALÉTIQUE ET DES SERVICES

Destiné à être joint à un dossier

Nom et prénoms C A V A N A G H, James   Nº d'inc. 7I.I37   Grade 2° Classe

Nationalité ANGLAISE   Titre ETRANGER

ÉTAT-CIVIL

Né le 22 Mai 1916   à STOKA STAFFORDSHIRE ton de

départ. d ANGLETERRE , résidence à   départ. d

Yeux Bleus

Cheveux Chatains

Front

Nez

Visage

Taille I m 74 cm

Marques particulières

Legionnaires breaking out of Bir Hakeim on the night of 10 June 1942

A legionnaire is decorated by General de Larminat after the battle of Bir Hakeim

Legionnaires escort Berber tribeswomen to a protected village in 1961

figures of the Legion. There was General Wrangel and his general staff from the Russian White Army, who formed the nucleus of a highly successful squadron of cavalry in the 1st REC, and Prince Christian Aage of Denmark, who joined the Legion in 1922 and who might have been the inspiration for the romanticism of P.C. Wren's classic novel, *Beau Geste*. Highly respected by his fellow officers and legionnaires, it was thought he might command the 13th Foreign Legion (Mountain) half-brigade (13th DBLE) in 1940 during the Norwegian campaign but he was seriously ill and died in February 1940, shortly before the half-brigade left for France.

During the 1930s the Legion and its doings were very much in the public eye, possibly arising from romantic novels of the time and the fact that it was a 'natural' for Hollywood film producers. An event that was to have considerable significance fifteen years hence was the formation on 1 September 1930 of the 5th Foreign Infantry Regiment (5th REI) from four Legion battalions of the 1st REI stationed in Indo-China, for which there was no shortage of recruits, as high unemployment brought forward many new entrants.

It was in this period that the centenary of the Legion occurred, in 1931, and General Paul Rollet had a most impressive war memorial built to honour the Legion's dead and to commemorate its anniversary, erected at the Quartier Viénot, Sidi-bel-Abbès. Rollet gave his second-in-command, Major Maire, the task of building the monument to the architect's design. With the authority of the Governor-General of Algeria, he re-opened an old onyx mine near the village of d'Oued-Chouly some forty miles (sixty-five kilometres) from Sidi-bel-Abbès, the legionnaires constructing a motor road linking the mine with the barracks. The foundation stone was laid on 8 October 1930 and the memorial completed on 10 March 1931, for the anniversary of the establishment of the Legion, but it was not dedicated until 30 April 1931 (the Fête de Camerone) in the presence of many honoured guests, including Prince Louis II of Monaco. This Monument to the Dead was transported to France in 1962 when the Legion left Algeria and re-erected at the Quartier Viénot in Aubagne, where it now stands. It cost 600,000 francs (£8,000) and was paid for by the legionnaires, NCOs and officers wherever they were stationed, on the basis of one day's pay per annum. The names of the contributors, more than 30,000, were enshrined in the masonry at the base of the monument.

On 14 September 1932 a detachment left Sidi-bel-Abbès for Morocco. Whilst passing through Tlemcen an explosion destroyed thirty wagons, many carrying ammunition, wounding 217 legionnaires and killing fifty-six, who were buried at Sidi-bel-Abbès on 16 September 1932.

General Rollet retired in 1936 with the title of Inspector-General of the Legion and died in Paris in 1941. His funeral was attended by General von Stulpnagel, the Commandant of German-occupied Paris, who had requested permission to attend 'as a great personal honour', so high was the esteem in which General Rollet had been held. His death brought to an end an era in the Legion's history, for the next twenty-five years were to see it involved in almost continuous fighting. First there was World War II and then the bitter struggle in Indo-China, quickly followed by the Algerian war, which was to end with the Legion leaving the Magrheb, its adopted homeland.

4 'A Moi la Légion'

The outbreak of World War II in September 1939 brought an influx of foreign residents in France, refugees and others who volunteered for service with the French Army. They were assimilated into three specially formed regiments of the Legion, the 21st, 22nd and 23rd Marching Regiments of Foreign Volunteers (RMVE), officered by French reservists. However, reservists were placed in two new infantry regiments, the 11th and 12th REI, with officers and NCOs from the active list. There was a view in the Legion that amongst the younger German recruits of the thirties were Nazi infiltrators, who were ruthlessly screened out at the outbreak of war and sent to Colomb-Bechar to patrol and build roads. However, before any of the newly created regiments was brought into action, a light mobile unit, the 97th Foreign Divisional Reconnaissance Group (GERD 97), was created to act in support, utilizing the second squadron of the 1st REC, although most of the officers and NCOs were drawn from the 2nd Foreign Cavalry Regiment (2nd REC) which was disbanded in the autumn of 1940, having been formed only on 1 July 1939.

At about the same time as the above events were taking place, the 13th Foreign Legion (Mountain) half-brigade (13th DBLE), commanded by Lieutenant-Colonel Magrin-Vernerey had been formed on 20 February 1940, at Sidi-bel-Abbès with one battalion. The word 'Mountain' was soon dropped from the title. A second battalion was raised at Fez, being united with the first to form the 13th DBLE on 27 February. The unit had 280 former Spanish Republican soldiers in its two battalions, mainly riflemen and mortar crews, who had fought in the Spanish Civil War but with short service in the Legion. They were considered by the Legion good fighters but poor soldiers. Magrin-Vernerey had told them in Fez,

'This is the Foreign Legion. It is not an International Legion.'
Assembling at Marseilles on 6 March 1940, the units original
destination had been Finland to support the Finns in their war
against the USSR, but that ceased before the Legion could take
part, to the evident relief of the Spaniards who had been supported
by the USSR in their civil war.

But war returned to Scandinavia in the spring of 1940, firstly
because of Norway's coastline in the strategy of the North Sea and
secondly Sweden's iron ore, much of which was exported to
Germany through Norway's ice-free port at Narvik. The Norwegian
Government adopted a policy of neutrality in the belief that
Britain's sea power would discourage a German invasion attempt –
a view shared by the British Chiefs of Staff, who considered an
invasion of Norway's western seaboard by Germany to be
impracticable. Whilst the Germans had their doubts too, Hitler
demanded it, and so on 7 April a fleet of warships carrying about
10,000 men sailed for Narvik, Trondheim, Bergen and Kristianland
– the supply ships having set out several days previously. To complete the attack, a parachute assault was to be made at Stavanger
and an air landing at the vital Sola airfield. After a stormy crossing
involving skirmishes with the Royal Navy and the Royal Air Force,
the weather-beaten German destroyers steamed up Ofotfjord for
Narvik, destroying two coastal defence vessels and landing their
troops together with the officer commanding, General Dietl, who
was able to persuade Colonel Sundlo, the Norwegian garrison
commander, to surrender and avoid useless bloodshed. Similar
landings took place at the other ports, and the surviving destroyers
withdrew. Shattered at the success of the Germans, the British
mounted a counter-invasion but by the end of April only Narvik
and the north of Norway remained as a theatre of operations, with
General Dietl holding out with an isolated group of 2,000 mountain
troops and a similar number of seamen survivors from the German
destroyers.

Major-General Mackesey commanded the British and Polish
forces who had landed on 15 April at Harstad on the Lofoten
Islands, north-west of Narvik, and to reinforce them the 13th DBLE
embarked at Brest on 20 April, sailing via Gourock to Norway on
the *Monarch of Bermuda* (a Canadian Pacific liner), on which the
legionnaires had their own cabins and in the officers' mess were
served by white-coated stewards. Supported by some artillery and a

few tanks, they landed on Sunday 5 May at Ballangen, the advanced base for operations at Narvik. On 11 May the Earl of Cork and Orrery, Admiral of the Fleet, was replaced as overall commander of the British, French and Polish forces by Lieutenant-General Auchinleck. Finding Général de Division Bethouart (who was in overall command of the French forces in Norway) preparing to act, he encouraged the developing relationship between the Legion and the Royal Navy, which resulted in British landing craft putting ashore the 13th DBLE supported by three French tanks at 01.00 hours on 13 May. The tanks proved useless, in view of the steepness of the coast, and elsewhere the legionnaires sank into the snow every few paces. Opposing German machine-gun fire was soon silenced, enabling the legionnaires to advance up the road to meet the Norwegians, Royal Navy gunfire having prepared the way for the legionnaires' landing. In a matter of hours, the 1st Battalion took Bjervik, a large village of wooden buildings at the north point of the fjord, and on the next day the 2nd Battalion completed the destruction of six German aircraft, partially submerged in the ice of Lake Hartvigvard, which had been observed by the 1st Battalion.

On 10 May the Germans had launched their invasion, which eventually engulfed most of Europe. However, for the Legion the fighting in Norway continued in support of the Norwegian Army, and in the early hours of 28 May, after a preliminary naval bombardment, the 13th DBLE and a battalion of Norwegians were landed from the five remaining landingcraft on the northern side of the Narvik peninsula. Beating off a German attack, one company of the 2nd Battalion, under Captain Szabo, advanced along the railway line linking Norway and Sweden to take Narvik despite fierce air and ground resistance which cost this company all its officers and six legionnaires. It was in this battle that Legionnaire James Williamson won the Croix de Guerre with bronze star, and the Barretts Norvège for overcoming a German defensive gun lodged in the railway tunnel. The seven captured German gunners were killed digging a grave for one of their comrades, when one of their own bombs landed amongst them. Meanwhile, the 1st Battalion pushed through the mountains, forcing the Germans back to their last mountain position despite their having been reinforced by parachute troops on 22 and 25 May. However, the end of resistance in central Norway had enabled Dietl to be reinforced with troops, which included the 11th Mountain Division.

Two captured German naval officers were executed by the legionnaires, and in another incident legionnaires shot the crew of a German aircraft which had force-landed and who had been captured by British troops. It appears that whilst under escort one German who had secreted a Luger pistol managed to shoot four and severely wound two of his British guards.

The Allied success was, however, overshadowed by the disastrous situation developing in France and the Low Countries, and plans for evacuation of Norway were in preparation before planning the capture of Narvik had been completed. This resulted in the last British and French forces embarking at Harstad on 8 June, the 13th DBLE having evacuated Narvik on 4 June, embarking at Harstad the next day, returning to Brest via Glasgow where they disembarked on Saturday 8 June to be greeted by the port officer, who told them, 'The Germans entered Paris this morning.'

Lieutenant-Colonel Magrin-Vernerey was a much-wounded veteran who had fought in the trenches of Flanders in World War I and was determined not to be beaten if he could do otherwise. He was a firebrand of a man (who suffered from acute hiccups); a harsh disciplinarian, he ordered that two legionnaires, brothers who were caught deserting to the enemy, be shot in full view of the whole battalion. At Brest he announced 'We shall fight on', and shortly afterwards is reputed to have shot dead, in the mess tent, a young French infantry lieutenant who told him, 'You'll only cause trouble for us if you don't lay down your arms.'

Reconnoitring the Liffre Forest near Rennes, Lieutenant-Colonel Magrin-Vernerey, Major Pierre Koenig and Captain Amilakvari returned to Brest to find the regiment had disappeared. The three officers then crossed in a small boat to Southampton, landing on 21 June and meeting up with legionnaires who had crossed over on 19 June to Plymouth, travelling by train to Trentham Park, near Stoke-on-Trent, where they arrived on Friday 21 June. (Before leaving France all their heavy weapons had been destroyed.) On arrival at Trentham Park, which was absolutely full, the legionnaires were billeted with other French troops, including the Alpine Riflemen, sailors, police, boy scouts, Sengalese etc. The Park was patrolled by men of the Guard Patrol working in pairs. On the first night they slept under trees, on the second they were given tents.

By a trick of fate, Legionnaire James Williamson was back in his home town, and he (and others) undertook to visit the nearby town, with nocturnal visits to relatives and the nearest fish-and-chip shop (from which he obtained supplies of food to bribe his sergeant) by the simple expedient of climbing over the iron railings at the main entrance. Although the British had prepared food and accommodation, such were the number of escapees arriving that for some it was not until the fourth day after their arrival that they received any issue of rations, which consisted of potatoes, cabbage and corned beef, which they cooked in old-style washing-boilers. Then a legionnaire had the bright idea of improving the stew with local venison, and so the deer in Trentham Park were shot and eaten.

On 30 June the legionnaires were reviewed by General Charles de Gaulle but there was considerable confusion amongst them when he put his proposition to them that they should 'throw in their lot with the Free French'. It must be remembered that this was June 1940, France had capitulated and Britain was anticipating a German invasion. French officers advised the legionnaires who had accepted a 500-franc enlistment bounty with the French Republic that to join de Gaulle would result in their being posted as deserters, with every possibility of being shot if captured. The 2nd Battalion, whose commander had been killed at Bjervik, however, chose to join the Free French on a six-month contract and temporarily took the designation 14th DBLE, reverting in November to 13th DBLE. Lieutenant-Colonel Magrin-Vernerey changed his name to Monclar to avoid reprisals to his family.

'Why six months and not for the duration of the war?', Captain Arnault asked 'Monclar' later.

'I didn't trust the Churchill-de Gaulle agreement. I knew I had enough in the pay-chest to keep the men going for six months,' he replied.

When James Williamson returned to Trentham Park on 1 July at 06.30 hours, he found that his fellow legionnaires had departed. Reporting to the British guardroom, he was told that the French (Vichy) Army was no longer recognized in Britain and that the best thing he could do was 'clear off, burn his uniform and get some civilian clothes'. This he did, joining the British Army but remaining on the Legion's list of deserters until he was officially discharged on 5 April 1966.

Forty legionnaires – all Spaniards – who refused to fight against the USSR were placed in Stafford prison. They, and other legion-naires and French troops who sought repatriation, sailed from Britain on a French ship, the *Meknes*, and many of them survived World War II, including John Yeowell's section commander, Lieu-tenant Vadat.

In the Battle of France, the first regiment into action was the 11th REI, which distinguished itself in the Verdun sector when it was almost completely wiped out during the heroic defence of Inor Wood against a German division.

'Why fight?' whispered the French soldiers as the legionnaires re-grouped after the battle. 'Why get yourselves killed before the armistice?'

'The Legion dies on its feet', a Belgian legionnaire shouted in reply.

Ordered to pull back, and on 18 June almost encircled at St-Germain-sur-Meuse, the heroic stand made by the 2nd Battalion enabled the remainder to withdraw on 20 June, prior to which Colonel Jean-Baptiste Robert, who could no longer stand and fight, finding his force under heavy German assault at Blenod-lès-Toul, had soaked the regimental standard in petrol and ordered a legion-naire to set it alight in anticipation of a last stand.

Of the 11th REI's original 3,000 men, fewer than 800 remained, and of these only 450 could march. The survivors fought on until the armistice, when they laid down their arms and the regiment was disbanded. Of the 700 legionnaires taken prisoner at Verdun, some 500 had made their way back to North Africa by the end of 1940 and formed an important part of General Lattre's army of 1943.

The 12th REI was subject to an ordeal by German artillery and air attack on 6 June 1940, in the area of Soissons which it was defending as part of the 8th Infantry Division. By the night of the next day, the regiment, which had lost a third of its strength, was surrounded. Only a few men were able to slip through the German line and retreat to the area of Limoges, where they remained until the armistice on 25 June 1940. Despite the personal courage of many of those who served in the three RMVEs, there had been little oppor-tunity to equip or train them properly. Faced with the highly trained and substantially armoured German invaders, they put up a spirited defence but were badly mauled and soon pushed into retreat.

In the aftermath of the armistice, which provided for France to be divided into a German-occupied zone of about two-thirds of the country, and a non-occupied zone with its seat of control at Vichy, it was necessary for the Legion to establish its relationship with the new regime. The terms of the armistice did not provide for German control of French colonies, but officials of various Reich agencies were empowered to carry out inspections and obtain information. For the Legion itself, there was the problem of those who had enlisted for 'the duration only' but who now found themselves in North Africa. Not unnaturally, there was a reluctance to release individuals, particularly as there was now a shortage of recruits. Those who pressed their requests too vigorously for a discharge thus soon found themselves despatched for a corrective disciplinary course at one or another of the Legion's Sahara labour camps. Not a very fair approach, might be the comment, but it was war and 'If you can't take a joke, you shouldn't have joined' appeared to be the official attitude. The 4th REI was disbanded on 14 November 1940, its personnel passing to the 2nd REI. Various other unit changes took place, and for the ensuing three years the Legion suffered from a shortage of recruits and equipment.

Even before the war the Reich Government had discouraged its young men from joining the Legion, and efforts were made to catch up with those who had done so. In fact, pressure was put on the Vichy Government to disband the Legion entirely. For its part, the Legion attempted to circumvent the attempts of the German inspectorate and used its best endeavours to post men to units well away from German eyes and influence.

Tonkin and Senegal proved to be useful repositories for such men, and on the North African continent the Sahara Desert Patrol Group and the two new Motorized Saharan Batteries formed at Ouargla in October 1940 and Fort Flatters in April 1941, served a similar purpose. Nevertheless, the Germans managed to catch up with some 2,000 legionnaires who, although given a rough reception and described as unpatriotic, were largely recruited into the Deutsche Afrika Corps (DAK), many serving in the crack 90th Light Division which fought bitterly with the 13th DBLE at Bir Hakeim.

During the time the 13th DBLE was stationed at Trentham Park, the legionnaires received standard British battle-dress, which they wore with the khaki French beret, but for their next operation, in Eritrea, they received British khaki drill and tropical helmets, having put away, for the time being, the cherished white kepi. Prior to this operation they were sent to Cameroon and Gabon as part of the 1st Free French Brigade, for re-training. Disembarking at Port Sudan, they took part in the British assault on Italian-held Eritrea. Going into action on 1 March 1941, and after several victories, they finally took the port of Massawa on 8 April 1941 from a garrison of 14,000 enemy troops. It was to be Monclar's last battle as a legionnaire, for de Gaulle drafted the 13th DBLE into Syria, which was held by the 80,000 Vichy French, including the 6th REI, and Monclar told de Gaulle that he would not fight Frenchmen, regardless of their politics. In 1948, with the rank of General but using his wartime assumed name of Monclar, he became Inspector of the Legion until succeeded in 1957 by General Lenauyeux, who had been appointed Commander of the Legion on 1 July 1955.

Rumours that the Vichy troops were about to change sides proved false, as the 13th DBLE found out when in front of Damascus it faced the 6th REI (formed on 2 September 1939 from battalions of the 1st and 2nd REI stationed in the Levant). It was a tragic battle as legionnaire fought legionnaire, but the 13th DBLE finally brought about the surrender of the Vichy forces on 14 July 1941. The only good factor was that the combatants treated wounded as legionnaires first, enemy second. After the battle, two officers and a thousand legionnaires joined the 13th DBLE, which formed a third battalion; the remainder were shipped to France, then to North Africa, where the 6th REI was disbanded on 1 January 1942, most of the remaining personnel going to the depleted 1st REI at Sidi-bel-Abbès. At the conclusion of the Eritrean campaign, the 13th DBLE was posted to Ismailia, Egypt, for operations in Palestine and Syria, and then back to Egypt in December 1941. From 1 October it had a new commanding officer, Lieutenant-Colonel Amilakvari, a Georgian nobleman who had served with the Legion since 1924, and in Norway as a captain in the 2nd Battalion.

The battle at Gazala, between 26 May and 22 June 1942, is one of the significant campaigns which affected the outcome of World War II. Fought in the Western Desert, it is reputed to have had practically all the many facets of military drama and war itself.

Early in 1942 the 8th Army commanders decided to construct extensive field fortifications to dominate an area roughly 1,060 miles (1,700 kilometres) square, contained within the limits of Gazala, Bir Hakeim, Bir el Gubi and Tobruk. An extensive minefield running almost forty-three miles (sixty-nine kilometres) south from the sea protected the western side of the defence area, within which a number of heavily defended 'boxes' had been constructed. Designed to hold a complete brigade group, each box was provisioned with the appropriate supplies of food, water and ammunition. The British even provided a large quantity of wine for the legionnaires, but it had been rendered undrinkable by exposure of the metal containers to the sizzling heat! The most important boxes were those held at Bir Hakeim (the Chiefs Well marked as a caravan crossroads on the edge of the Libyan desert) by the Free French forces, consisting of the 13th DBLE, four colonial battalions and one marine battalion, together with another held by the British 150th Brigade Group of 50th (Northumberland) Division.

Arriving at the six-sided box on 14 February 1942, General Koenig, the French Commander-in-Chief, ordered his 3,300 men to dig in – and they did, constructing 1,200 slit trenches, gunpits and command posts. There was to be a second line of similar posts, but this was still under construction in mid-May. Unfortunately, the positions at Tobruk had been allowed to fall into neglect, but such reliance was placed on the first fortifications at Gazala that this was not considered important. Even more regrettable was the fact that this reliance was misplaced and the multiplicity of purposes their positions were supposed to serve had required the lifting of the minefields and other barriers in the Tobruk area to make up for shortages in equipment.

Colonel-General Rommel commanded the Panzerarmee Afrika, which consisted of German and Italian troops with armoured, motorized and infantry formations. Of particular interest was the German 90th Light Division, which had in its ranks a substantial number of former legionnaires. Rommel's plan was for a frontal holding attack, whilst the main assault was delivered by the Deutsches Afrika Corps (DAK) in a wide sweep around the southern end of the so-called Gazala line, with the objective of taking Tobruk in a twenty-four-hour push.

Rommel himself led the three armoured formations of the DAK, together with the Italian XXX Corps, towards Bir Hakeim. The not-unexpected assault commenced late in the evening of 26 May, and in the early hours of 27 May Rommel's troops were fighting at Bir Hakeim. All did not go his way, and the Italian Ariete armoured division's initial assault was driven off, after thirty tanks had been blown up in the minefield or destroyed by the 75mm guns within half an hour of their arrival. Although six tanks forced their way into the box, crushing a Legion command post, they were destroyed by legionnaires who thrust grenades under the visors and shot the fleeing crews. In all, thirty-five tanks were destroyed and, besides many dead, ninety-one prisoners were taken – all for one slightly scratched legionnaire! Further problems arose for Rommel, and his position became precarious when the German supply columns failed to appear – in particular the XV Panzer, which was dangerously low on fuel. For those defending the box, water was rationed to three pints (1.7 litres) per day in shade temperatures of 120°F (49°C). No one wore a shirt – the heat and sweat cracked them in a couple of hours. Rommel's next move was psychological: at dawn on 28 May he called on the defenders of Bir Hakeim to surrender, sending in a British soldier captured two days previously with a note signed by Rommel. Koenig's reply was to open fire immediately on all German vehicles in sight.

However, changing his tactics, which resulted in the destruction of the 150th Brigade box on 1 June, made Rommel more secure, and on 2 June he sent two Italian officers as emissaries to demand the surrender of the encircled troops to which request General Koenig sent the reply, 'I'm very sorry, gentlemen. Go and tell your general that we're not here to surrender.' An hour later the Germans attacked again from the north and the east, with the whole of the Italian 101st (Trieste) Division, parts of the German 17th and 27th Divisions and fifty tanks. Afterwards, Rommel sent a note in his own hand asking for surrender:

> To the troops of Bir Hakeim,
> All further resistance would lead only to useless bloodshed. You would suffer the same fate as the two British brigades located at Got Valeb, which were annihilated the day before yesterday. We will stop fighting as soon as you hoist the White Flag and come over to us unarmed.
> Rommel, Colonel-General

After this was refused, Koenig dictated the following order of the day:

> General Order:
> 1. We must now expect serious attack combining all resources (aircraft, tanks, artillery, infantry). It will be powerful.

2. I repeat my orders and my certainty that each man will do his duty without flinching in the place allotted to him, whether cut of from others or not.

3. Our task is to hold at all costs until our victory is assured.

4. Explain this clearly to all, both NCOs and men.

5. Good luck to you all.

Headquarters, 3 June, 9.30 a.m.   Koenig

Attacks by artillery and the Luftwaffe then increased in severity, although the Desert Air Force made the Luftwaffe pay dearly for these raids. At 04.30, during the next lull, Rommel sent two German officers to demand surrender, but again it was refused, so he launched another major attack involving the XV Panzer supported by dive bombers, the Italian Trieste Division and the 90th Light Division. However, he still did not overcome the defences and later wrote of his own troops, and in particular the 90th Light Division who bore the brunt of the attack: 'Yet for all their dash, this attack too was broken up by the fire of all arms. Only in the north were a few penetrations made. This was a remarkable achievement on the part of the French defenders, who were now completely cut off from everyone ... When my storming parties went in the next morning, the French opened fire again with undiminished violence. The enemy troops hung on grimly in their trenches and remained completely invisible.'

By 9 June supplies of all kinds, in particular ammunition, were running out, although until then occasional convoys had reached them overland, but on that day it was found necessary to drop supplies by air, and on the night of 10/11 June Koenig was authorized to break out. Helped by the 7th Motorized Brigade, the vanguard of 2,000 men got away to the east without interference, but the rearguard, which was trying to bring out its guns, was intercepted.

Although the night was dark and misty, the Germans illuminated the fifty-yard-wide corridor with flares, and there was fierce hand-to-hand fighting in the dark, with the German artillery, particularly the deadly 88mm guns, appearing to destroy the half-tracks and bren-carriers one by one. In the midst of this chaos, Lieutenant-Colonel Amilakvari and Captain Lamaze rallied their men with the traditional cry, 'A moi la Légion', but Lamaze was killed with a rifle in one hand and a grenade in the other.

Driving through the darkness at 40 mph, General Koenig's

British driver, Susan Travers (the daughter of a British admiral who had joined the Free French Army of Liberation in 1940 with the rank of sergeant), avoided the shell-holes by responding to foot signals from the general, who was travelling with her, balancing on her shoulders with his head projecting through the sliding roof of the car, which was eventually found to have eleven bullet-holes in it. Several times attacked by enemy troops, they lost touch with the others but they and the other survivors of the Free French Brigade filtered back through the 8th Army lines over the next three days. The break-out had been costly: seventy-two known dead and 763 missing – captured, killed or wounded, including thirty-three officers, although some 2,700 out of the original 3,600 made their escape. Half of the Gazala line had ceased to exist, and it was only matter of time before the battle went in Rommel's favour, although the epic fourteen-day stand of the French forces had caused him to delay by several days his main assault on Tobruk and the road to Egypt.

After the war a Paris Metro station on Line 8 was named 'Bir Hakeim' as a permanent reminder of the epic struggle, as was a boulevard in Marseilles.

Subsequently General Koenig received the DSO from General Alexander and Miss Travers the Croix de Guerre 1939-45, to which she added two citations, the Military Medal and the Colonial Medal some years later. By January 1944 she had become a Warrant Officer (1) attached to the 13th DBLE and participated in campaigns in Palestine, Levant, Libya, Egypt and France, finishing the war attached to the 1st Battalion of the RMLE. She then served in Indo-China, leaving the service in June 1947, after having married a Warrant Officer (1) of the 13th DBLE the previous April.

At El Alamein, on the night of 23/24 October 1942, the 13th DBLE was again in the thick of the fighting, having been given the task, together with a flying column of Spahis, of seizing El Himeimat, a triangular peak that dominated the sector from the south. In the first attack Lieutenant-Colonel Amilakvari was killed by a shell- burst. Subsequently the legionnaires penetrated $2\frac{1}{2}$ miles (four kilometres) beyond the hill, and the next morning they repelled two counter-attacks, at the same time immobilizing considerable forces. Having done their job, they withdrew.

By the end of the war in Tunisia, the 13th DBLE was down to 1,000 men, but with an influx of veterans from Algeria and

Morocco, and newly equipped, it joined the Allied forces in Italy in April 1944.

On 8 November 1942, a fortnight after the opening of the British offensive at El Alamein, Allied forces landed in Morocco and Algeria. Known as 'Operation Torch', it was recognized early in the planning stage that there were major problems to be solved with the French, and despite secret negotiations confusion arose over the Allied troops once ashore. At certain places there was resistance, at others co-operation, but fortunately the cease-fire ordered by Admiral Darlan was adhered to, despite a countermanding order sent to him by the Vichy Government.

If the Allies had not succeeded in enlisting Darlan's support, a difficult problem would have resulted, insofar as 120,000 French troops were based in North Africa at that time and would have presented a formidable resistance. Fortunately they chose the Allied cause, and on 23 March 1943 the 1st Foreign Infantry Marching Regiment (1st REIM) was formed from troops at Sidi-bel-Abbès and the 4th DBLE from Senegal. A small mobile group, formed from survivors of the 1st REC, consisting of one armoured car squadron and one infantry squadron, was the first unit to see action when, on 11 January 1943, it attacked and drove back the enemy at Foum-el-Gouafel, taking 200 prisoners and thirty 47mm guns. Early in May the 1st REIM (which included legionnaires from the 6th REI who had elected to be repatriated in 1941) suffered heavy casualties when, with British forces, it clashed with General von Arnim's tanks at Djebel Mansour. As the advance continued, the 1st REIM was committed, and it distinguished itself at Pont du Fahs and Djebel Zaghouan on 9 May. By the time the cease-fire came in North Africa on 11 May 1943, the regiment had taken some 5,000 prisoners. It was disbanded on 3 June 1943, its effectives joining elements from the disbanded 3rd REI to form an RMLE on 1 July, at Sidi-bel-Abbès inheriting the traditions of World War I and the flag of the 3rd REI.

The French Army in Africa was then re-organized and re-equipped by the Americans into five divisions, the 1st, 2nd and 5th being armoured. The RMLE provided the mechanized infantry for the 5th Armoured division, the 1st REC equipped with new American equipment formed part of the 5th Armoured Cavalry. Also re-equipped and re-organized was the 13th DBLE, which landed in April 1944 in Naples, Italy. Quickly finding itself in the fighting to pierce the Adolf Hitler Line (which was achieved on 25 May), it cleared the way through to Rome. Then the legionnaires had a brief respite until 15 June, when the 13th DBLE successfully fought against the Germans at Radicofani, where the advance had been halted by a defensive position in a Renaissance castle at the top of a sheer cliff that stood undefended. Lieutenant Julian and five volunteer legionnaires scaled the cliff and attacked the Germans from the rear whilst their comrades made a frontal diversionary attack. Acting simultaneously, they caused the three officers and ninety men to surrender.

Meanwhile, a bitter battle was being fought between the Allied leaders in regard to the invasion of Europe, where the Americans and Russians but not the British desired a landing in southern France in addition to the landings planned for the north. In fact, the decision to invade southern France was one of the most controversial decisions of World War II, and General Clark, the American Commander in Europe, described the operation as one of the 'outstanding political mistakes of the war'. Briefly, it allowed the Russians to occupy central Europe, whereas this chance might have gone to the Western powers if the momentum of the advance through Italy had been maintained.

General de Gaulle, ever mindful of the honour of France and having a desire for an equal voice in strategic decisions involving French forces, requested their withdrawal from the Mediterranean command on 25 July in readiness for their transfer to France, even though General Tuim, the commander of the French Expeditionary force to Italy, objected to de Gaulle for the reasons outlined in the previous paragraph. For France it meant that French-led troops took a full share in the Liberation, and the view of those taking part was summed up in the message sent to the commander of the French commandos about to land: 'The Admiral, officers and crew of the Allied Fleet salute Lieutenant-Commander Bouvet and his men, who will have the honour of being the first to set foot on their native shores and to liberate and protect them. May God guard and protect them.'

At the time of the landing, French forces were under American control, but once the two corps were in the field, this control passed to General de Lattre de Tassigny as part of the command structure. The first legionnaires ashore were the 13th DBLE, who landed at Cavalaire at 18.00 hours on 16 August and fought a difficult battle to clear the Hyères saltmarshes and the area of Carqueiranne.

The Bas Fort St-Nicholas at Marseilles which was to become for many years the Legion's 'transit camp' (in place of Fort St-Jean which had been destroyed by the Germans) for recruits *en route* to Africa was liberated by Goums of General Guillaume's 4th Moroccan Mountain Division.

Advancing rapidly along the course of the River Rhône to Lyons, which was reached on 5 September, de Lattre had to assert himself to make sure French troops were not accorded secondary roles. This was certainly the case on 9 September when, in face of stiffening German resistance, the legionnaires had to fight for Autun yard by yard. Moving north-westwards, the 13th DBLE met up with their comrades from the RMLE and the 1st REC (both of whom had landed at Toulon in late September 1944) at Haute-Saône, prior to attacking the well-defended German positions in and around Belfort, Alsace. (It was here that the 13th DBLE incorporated into its ranks a battalion of White Russians serving with the Wehrmacht!) Next month the 13th DBLE were switched to the Atlantic coast to reduce a number of stubborn German pockets of resistance, returning to Alsace to take part in the defence of Strasbourg during the German counter-offensive in the Ardennes (the Battle of the Bulge).

At Colmar the 13th DBLE joined up with the RMLE, which reached and crossed into Germany on 20 March, reaching Stuttgart on 21 April and the River Danube at Tuttingen on 25 April 1945, and its first battalion the Arlberg on 6 May 1945. Meanwhile the 13th DBLE had moved into the Alps, where they seized the Authion Mountains and had opened the Col di Tende pass to Italy by the time of the cease-fire on 8 May 1945.

A foretaste of other problems which lay in store occurred on 10 May 1945, when a bloody uprising broke out in the region of Setif, Algeria, where the rising tide of nationalism in North Africa almost brought civil war to Algeria in 1947. Prisoners-of-war were released and armed to assist the Legion. Many took the short cut to freedom and enlisted at Sidi-bel-Abbès. Although the situation was contained, the desire for change was evident. Meanwhile, in Tunisia and Morocco, where theoretically France's role was that of a protectorate power, the local administrators had been reduced to the status of a puppet government, and French refusal to allow participation and autonomy gave the struggle for nationalism its strength. In the aftermath of World War II, when France was endeavouring to regain its lost credibility, the fact that independence was inevitable was not even considered but in 1950 Bourguiba (later President of Tunisia) was to write: 'It is not a question of choosing between independence under guidance with freedom of co-operation ... and winning independence by means of hate and bloodshed.' There was scope for compromise, but the French Government was not prepared to take part in the formation of a gradual partnership, thereby bypassing a unique opportunity and simultaneously encouraging the strengthening of the emergent nationalists.

At the conclusion of World War II, the Legion, although much reduced in numbers, had emerged as a highly trained combat group, as opposed to its pre-war role as a colonial pacification force. It is unfortunate that the higher echelons of the French military establishment had not the opportunity, or perhaps the will, to absorb the new developments, a factor which was to have a profound effect on the conduct of the forthcoming struggle in Indo-China.

5 *Honneur et Fidélité*

Obeying orders from Paris, the 5th REI (the Regiment of Tonkin) did not resist the Japanese invasion in 1940 and subsequent occupation of Indo-China. There were no serious incidents, and an uneasy peace lasted until early in 1945 when General Emile Lemonnier (the French commander of the Lang Son area) received an official invitation requesting the honoured presence of the Lang Son garrison to a banquet in the Imperial Japanese Army's divisional headquarters during the evening of 9 March 1945. After some deliberation, General Lemonnier allowed a number of his officers to attend the banquet, where they were greeted with Oriental courtesy and escorted to the banqueting hall where a band was playing Western jazz music. At precisely 20.00 hours the music stopped, a Japanese officer shouted an order, and the French found themselves looking into revolver muzzles. Those who resisted were shot or run through with Samurai swords.

General Lemonnier and the French resident, Camille Auphalle, were taken prisoner and presented with a surrender document. Called upon to sign, Lemonnier cried out, 'Never', whereupon he and Auphalle were taken to the Kiluo grottoes near the Chinese border and forced to dig their own graves. Kneeling before them, they again refused to sign, and both were beheaded on the spot. Japanese forces then attacked the posts and forts at Ha Giang, Lang Son and Hanoi, the legionnaires fighting with bayonets when their ammunition was exhausted, but overwhelming numbers defeated their brave actions and several lived to be taken prisoner. These unfortunate men were lined up against a wall, shot in the feet, then killed by the Japanese whilst they lay wounded on the ground, the murderers using bayonets, swords, gun butts, knives and even picks to finish them off.

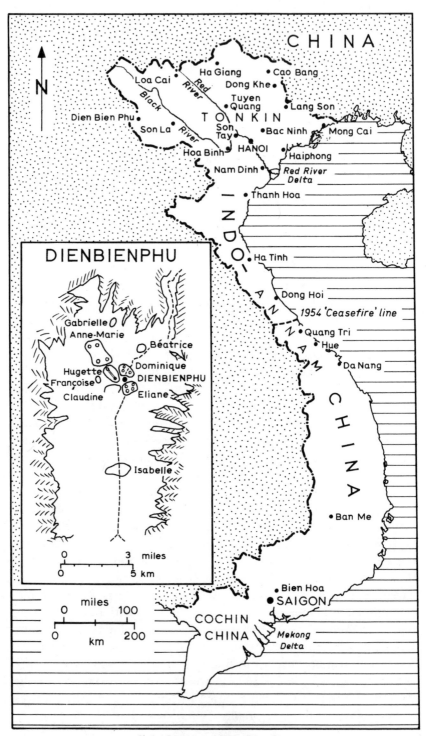

Indo-China and Dien Bien Phu

But there were survivors, mainly a large detachment of the 5th REI who received the news of the death of their comrades whilst on column near the Red River. Under the command of Colonel Marcel Alessandri and Captains Gaucher, Guy de Cockbourne and Raoul Lenior, a fighting retreat was planned through some 500 miles (800 kilometres) of jungle to Chinese territory. Leaving Indo-China, which legionnaires had regarded as 'their country' since arriving there on 8 November 1883, was a great blow worsened by the order that civilians would not be evacuated with them. For many, this meant leaving behind their *congai* – Vietnamese girls who faithfully served them as wives and mistresses. Many a tough legionnaire had been tamed by the fragile beauty who ran his home and gave him a family life. One girl named Moona defied the order and trailed the battalion for 150 miles (240 kilometres) through the jungle to be reunited with Sergeant Leibner. Tragedy struck when he was killed in a skirmish with the Japanese, and Moona, after gazing at his body, vanished without trace into the surrounding jungle.

The withdrawal was continually harassed by the Japanese but the legionnaires fought them off. After existing on a spoonful of meat and a handful of rice a day, suffering from beri-beri and walking in bare feet, they crossed into Yunnon on 2 May 1945. General Zinovi Pechkoff, a hero of the Legion, was French Ambassador to the Government of General Chiang Kai Chek, and through his good offices the wounded and sick were evacuated to India, whilst the remainder were re-mustered to form an independent *bataillon de marche* of the 5th REI, the regiment itself having been disbanded on 1 July, 1945. On 8 February 1946 they commenced a march back south along a route which followed the Tonkin-Laos border, later to become famous as 'the Red Highway' or 'Ho Chi Minh trail'. Apart from the difficult terrain, a series of skirmishes were fought with local bandits who had flourished during the power-vacuum which occurred towards the end of World War II, and it was with some difficulty that the battalion managed to reach Laos and the Mekong Valley.

With the war in Europe at an end, the French Government was establishing a division based at St-Raphaël, which included a regiment of the Legion, to take part in the final attack on Japan. On 1 July 1945 it received the title Marching Regiment of the Foreign Legion in the Far East (RMLE-EO) and, with a nucleus of experienced legionnaires, training of new recruits from Germany, Italy and France commenced at Sidi-bel-Abbès. However, before it was committed, the war with Japan ceased, in August 1945, and within the terms of the Potsdam Conference as part of the peace arrangements Indo-China was partitioned into occupation zones, the north to China, the south to Britain.

But the post-war French Government was determined not to give up an inch of its territory or power. Perhaps it was to recover faded glory, perhaps it was in response to vested interests: the reasons have never been clearly stated.

To re-assert French influence, the RMLE-EO was re-designated the 2nd RE on 1 January 1946 and dispatched to Indo-China, the legionnaires disembarking at Saigon in South Annam on 2 February.

These units were joined in April and June by the 3rd REI, and between them they undertook pacification duties in the three provinces of Indo-China, namely Annam in the centre, Cochin-China in the south, Tonkin in the north, and along the border ridges. The disposition was four independent battalions grouped along the frontier with China from Mong Cai to Lao Cai connected by RC4 (Route Coloniale no. 4) which for sixty years had served the area for strategic, economic and tourist purposes. In March 1946 the 13th DBLE had landed and, in addition to pacification duties in Cochin China and South Annam, it restored order in Saigon, in conjunction with the *bataillon de marche* of the 5th REI, which returned to Sidi-bel-Abbès in November 1946, where it was disbanded on 20 January 1947.

If the French Government regarded the return of the Legion to Indo-China as a repeat of the earlier pacification measures, others had a different view, for opposing the Japanese during their occupation had been the Viet Minh guerrillas. This movement had originated in 1941 at the Chinese town of Tienshui and, with the support of American weapons and advisers, together with a promise of post-war self-determination, had valiantly fought the Japanese invaders. With the withdrawal of the British and Nationalist Chinese, the French returned and in 1946 established in the south the corrupt regime of the morally weak traditional Prince of Annam, Bao Dai, who had, at the request of the Japanese in 1945, denounced the French protectorate. With the returning French presence, Ho Chi Minh considered he had been betrayed, and he established a popular government in the north within the French Union, calling every Indo-Chinese patriot together under the flag of Liberation – 'Come to us, regardless of your political beliefs or social status' – and they came.

There was no prospect of uniting north and south, and although the elections of 1946 returned both Communists and non-Communists, it was the Communists who held the key positions. A hundred thousand people gathered in Hanoi's main square on 8 November 1946 to celebrate the birth of the Democratic Republic of Vietnam (DRV), and amongst the guests of honour were American officers and representatives of the Russian and Chinese Governments. Ho Chi Minh was elected as first President and, following the rules of all Communist dictators, started to eliminate the opposition whilst endeavouring at the same time to maintain friendly relations with the French. To emphasize Ho Chi Minh's determination, a few 'pin-prick' guerrilla attacks were mounted against the French, but after two incidents when the Viet Minh killed twenty-nine French soldiers, a massive retaliatory bombardment of Hai Phong late in November 1946 by a French cruiser caused 6,000 civilian casualties. This brought about a Viet Minh reprisal on 19 December in Hanoi, when 600 French civilians were killed or abducted, so the French set out to capture Ho Chi Minh and eliminate the Viet Minh. In retaliation, Vo N'Guyen Giap assembled his guerrillas, who exterminated French garrisons in the south.

The result was predictable: the Foreign Legion invaded the north, Ho Chi Minh withdrew into China, and the Viet Minh took to the hills to prepare for the forthcoming struggle. The method employed by Lyautey in Morocco was being used to control the three provinces in Indo-China (see Chapter 3, page 49). Several thousand defence posts were built. These initially consisted of a rectangular enclosure measuring about thirty to forty yards (twenty-four to thirty-two metres) surrounded by a rough wall of stones, breeze blocks or wooden stakes. At the centre of the courtyard was the flagpole and beside it the mortar pit. The courtyard was the social centre of the post, and at some of them, against the outer wall, were such buildings as the commander's room, barracks, food store, ammunition magazine and armoury. Larger posts had a dining-hall, a sick-bay and a prison. Perhaps the ultimate post was the headquarters of the 13th DBLE at Hoc Monh, built and designed entirely by the legionnaires, constructed of red brick with its own electricity, proper plumbing and sanitation, which enabled the legionnaires to fight hard but live comfortably.

For defence, a blockhouse stood at each corner and was protected by sandbags, stakes or whatever was available. At some posts the range of vision was increased by means of a 'look-out tower' which took on the function of the keep in a medieval castle. It was at posts like this that the Viet Minh and the Legion fought most of their battles, and in the bitter struggles many of the 'look-out towers' were defended to the end – the ultimate place of resistance.

French tactics, and in particular those of the Legion, appear to have been centred at this time on warfare in the deserts of North Africa, where recruits received comprehensive training in conventional combat strategy. Their generals fought the battles as though they were in the fields of France or the Sahara, considering themselves too dignified to read Mao Tse-tung's doctrine on guerrilla warfare. The French chose to regard the fighting as just another colonial pacification campaign, and it was not until 1950 that they began to appreciate that it was a new kind of war. The Viet Minh, however, followed Soviet and Chinese guerrilla strategy, and it was comparatively easy for them to function in the atmosphere caused by the confused military, political, economic and social chaos which constituted the French colonial administration in Indo-China. Even the French maps were inaccurate, and experienced Legion officers, particularly the Germans, often preferred to use old wartime Japanese maps. Corruption was the way of life in the south, where numerous political leaders and religious sects, all with private armies, some numbering 20,000 men, fought each other, the French and the Viet Minh and, when convenient, switched sides. Their country was of no consequence to them, only the money which could be made. It was a perfect example of the chaotic French administration which welcomed back the renegades, when they decided to switch back to the French – instead of disarming, trying and hanging them.

In January 1946 the 1st REC had landed and fought on foot in central Annam, until April 1947, when it received sufficient British and US armoured fighting vehicles to equip two squadrons. Later in the year other units were similarly equipped, the final deliveries taking place in December. The 1st and 2nd Squadrons had considerable success with security operations in the swamps of the Plain of Tumba using US M29 'Crab' and 'Alligator' amphibious vehicles.

The need for skilled troops was filled by recruiting large numbers of World War II veterans, many German. Legionnaires trained in Africa needed at least a year to become expert anti-guerrilla fighters in the jungles of Asia, but the Germans were highly experienced in this type of warfare and able to adapt to the country without sustaining serious losses. At first they were placed in mixed battalions, in conformity with the normal procedures of the Legion, but in 1948 all German troops were properly screened and re-grouped into a battalion of approximately 900 men in three companies. With their own officers, many who had achieved restoration of their comparable German ranks, they were given maximum support and attempted to achieve the impossible; whether they lived or died was not important to the French.

The North African and mixed troops of the Legion, whilst being magnificent, brave and tenacious soldiers, lacked proper food, medical care, sufficient ammunition and reinforcements. The locally raised Vietnamese units were not given the full range of Legion uniform, in particular the kepi or the blue sash, although Asians who joined in the normal way were not subject to such discrimination. Sent without appropriate training to fight an unconventional war in the jungles and swamps of Indo-China, it was not only the ferocious attacks of the Viet Minh which caused them to have fifty per cent casualties but the physical hazards of animals, snakes and disease which took their toll as they tried to penetrate the green sea of bamboo and lianas. As their comrades died, the survivors were re-grouped, sent back into the fight and decimated again until they were wiped out. Hostilities did not develop as a series of major battles across the landmass but evolved as a seesaw war of guerrilla and anti-guerrilla operations. To meet this threat France responded by increasing the number of combat troops, and to provide a source of manpower the 6th REI was reformed in 1949 and stationed in Tunisia.

To win the struggle against the Viet Minh meant winning the minds of the people and, pursuing this policy, the legionnaires attempted to gain the villagers' confidence by involving themselves in the life of the community. They opened schools, built roads, established markets and became amateur judges, administrators, schoolteachers and doctors. The Viet Minh for their part posed as gallant freedom fighters but tortured and killed for the sheer pleasure of causing pain and seeing blood. Not only were the French their victims: so were their own countrymen if they did not accept the policy of Ho Chi Minh. They were fearless and tenacious fighters, and the Legion accepted no prisoners, speaking to them in the only language they understood – the machine-gun. The policy of kindness to the community was abandoned in the face of Communist brutality, which turned Indo-China into a slaughter-house, where cruelty became the norm. The combatants were not content to kill one another: they had to indulge in torture and butchery.

Near Saigon, the Viet Minh crucified seventeen legionnaires from the 3rd REI. Before nailing the men to the crosses, they slit their skin across their backs so that, as they slid down the crucifixes, the skin was stripped off, condemning the victims to a slow, agonizing death. Another favourite was to impale the victims on bamboo chairs, the spikes entering their bodies one more inch each day; others were covered in honey and left to the attention of giant red ants.

George Robert Elford, in his book *Devil's Guard,** quotes another incident which involved the battalion of German legionnaires, many of whom were former Waffen SS Partisan Jaeger – guerrilla hunters who had fought the Russian partisans in World War II. When they moved into Communist-dominated territory, they brought peace, often the peace of death brought about by their guns or bayonets.

> Near Hoa Binh we discovered the mutilated corpses of two German legionnaires. Both men had been disembowelled and castrated, with their private parts cut away and placed in their hands. A macabre Viet Minh joke.
>
> Two days later we captured the four terrorists responsible for the murder and mutilation. They were stripped and a thin cord was fastened around their private parts and with the other end tied to the jeep. The vehicle was driven at a speed the prisoners could pace by easy running and so avoid having their testicles torn from their

* Reprinted by permission of New English Library Ltd.

bodies. In such fashion we brought them to the dead legionnaires, about two miles down the road. Then the driver shifted gears and accelerated. The jeep sprang forward and the prisoners tumbled. Screaming in agony they rolled in the dust. We bayonetted them as they lay bleeding. The score was settled.

Accepting the need for greater mobility, the Legion experimented with a para company formed within the 3rd REI during April 1948, which was followed up in May with the formation of a parachute instruction centre at Khamisis, near Sidi-bel-Abbès. 1 July saw the establishment of a Legion parachute battalion, the 1st Foreign Parachute Battalion (1st BEP) under the command of Captain (later Major) Segrétain who was killed in action at Cox Xa. Sent to Indo-China in November, it absorbed the 3rd REI's para company in June, 1949. Following the success of the airborne forces which formed an important part of the mobile reserve in combatting the outbreaks of guerrilla warfare, the Legion expanded its parachute capability by raising the 2nd Foreign Parachute Battalion (2nd BEP), which followed the 1st BEP to Indo-China in February 1949, becoming involved in operations from Saigon and making seven combat drops in South Annam and Cambodia. A third battalion, the 3rd BEP, was formed in Algeria to provide replacements for the two combat battalions.

By 1948 the guerrilla activities had escalated from relatively small-scale terrorism to attacks on French convoys, although their forts were not generally attacked. These so called 'low-intensity' operations were costly, and the 2nd REI lost 230 men killed or wounded in only three months of security operations against a weak and poorly organized enemy. However, Vo N'Guyen Giap was learning, and the commander of the fort at Phu Tong Hoa on the Cao Bang range, Captain Cardinal, had increased the number of patrols to observe the large concentrations of Viet Minh forces in the area.

The legionnaires lived in combat order with their weapons beside them, and at 19.30 hours on 25 July 1948 the 316th Viet Minh division opened fire on the fort with mortars and 75mm and 37mm guns. To the command 'Take post', the 104 legionnaires of the first battalion of the 3rd REI manned their positions, but at 20.05 a well-aimed shot killed Captain Cardinal, and fifteen minutes later the second-in-command, Lieutenant Charlotton, suffered the same fate, leaving in charge Second Lieutenant Bevalot, who had landed in Indo-China only a few days previously. The radio-operator informed him that he had alerted the post at Bac Tan, who would do their best to help, but immediately afterwards the radio aerial was destroyed, and Phu Tong Hoa was incommunicado. At 21.00 the enemy artillery fire ceased, to be replaced by the sound of bugles that heralded and then accompanied waves of attacking Viet Minh, yelling as they charged, '*Tien Len, Anh Hai! Doc Lap! Di Di Moulen*' ('On, on, elder brother! On, on at the double! Uncle Ho will live for a thousand years'). They came from three directions, breaching the western perimeter to fight hand to hand for half an hour, piling up their corpses over which they climbed until by sheer force of numbers they entered the post. Sergeant Huegin, with a light machine-gun, fought them off alone for a quarter of an hour. Paulen, the radio-operator, who went to help him, was killed with a bayonet, and at 22.00 hours Huegen died. But the legionnaires had their cry too, 'Forward the Legion.' 'At hand-to-hand they're not worth a light.' At the point of the bayonet they drove the Viet Minh back across the courtyard. It was Camerone all over again. But luck was on their side. Shortly after midnight the clouds rolled back, the moonlight illuminating the battlefield, and out of the night came the call of a bugle – a Viet Minh bugle – sounding the withdrawal. Fighting only in darkness, the moon upset them, and by 01.00 the legionnaires had cleaned up the last of the enemy.

Second Lieutenant Bevalot did not know that a relief column was fighting its way from Bac Tan, and it was not until two days later that it arrived under the command of Colonel Simon. Although two officers and twenty-one NCOs and men were dead and the post was three-quarters destroyed, Simon was amazed to see the tricolour at the top of the flagpole, the post cleaned up and the garrison of the police post paraded in uniform with belts, epaulettes and kepis.

It was this battle which determined French policy to swamp the guerrillas with manpower represented by an Expeditionary Force of 50,000 regular troops including Navy and Air Force detachments, supported by 25,000 African sharpshooters, 5,000 irregulars, Thais etc and some 20,000 legionnaires. However, although the enemy at this time was numerically inferior, the employment by the French military and civil administration of large numbers of the indigenous population provided Ho Chi Minh with a highly successful intelligence organization, which worked to the great disadvantage of the French.

Vo N'Guyen Giap received a great boost to the development of his regular army when the Communist victory in China in the autumn of 1949 gave the Viet Minh an ally and supplier already skilled in the art of conventional and guerrilla warfare. Soon weapons, equipment and instructors began to cross the border for distribution by way of the Ho Chi Minh trail. The French High Command seemed to share none of the fears of the legionnaires at the policy of attempting to control the Viet Minh by limiting the French forces to the main towns, roads and forts, leaving control of most of the country at night to the guerrillas. The Viet Minh view was expressed by Ho Chi Minh in 1946: 'The enemy will pass slowly from the offensive to the defensive. The Blitzkreig will transform itself into a war of long duration. Thus the enemy will be caught in a dilemma. He has to drag out the war in order to win it and does not possess, on the other hand, the psychological and political means to fight a long drawn-out war.'

The French need for further troops led to the reformation of the 5th REI by battalions during 1949-50. This was undertaken in Tonkin, and some of the legionnaires were locally recruited.

By this time, Vo N'Guyen Giap was able to put up six regular divisions into the attack against the important post at Dong Khe, situated midway on the Cao Bang Ridge. Despite an heroic struggle by legionnaires of the 3rd Battalion of the 3rd REI, the post was overrun on 17 September 1950, giving the advantage to Giap. Attacking with such ferocity, the Viet Minh forced the defenders to seek refuge in the surrounding jungle, where the French were soon destroyed.

General Giap's next potential obstacle was the solidly built Legion fort at Cao Bang. Although the French High Command had not then conceived the idea of isolated 'airheads' (highly fortified areas supplied entirely by air), Colonel Charton, the officer commanding Cao Bang, and General Alessandri (who had commanded the French column which escaped from the Japanese in March 1945) wanted to stand and fight. Their superior, General Carpentier, decided otherwise and on 15 September 1950 ordered Colonel Charton to evacuate Cao Bang. This he followed by another order: 'We will evacuate admittedly, but with honour.'

So it was not to be an airlift but a march by 200 men for fifty miles (eighty kilometres) along a road controlled by the Viet Minh.

To assist the withdrawal, a relief column, the Bayard Group, was to rendezvous with Charton's troops. The only redeeming feature was the presence of the 1st BEP with the Bayard Group, which consisted of North Africans commanded by an almost time-served colonel named Bayard. Towards the end of September the order arrived from Saigon: 'Evacuate Cao Bang on 3 October. Do not destroy equipment so as not to alert the Viet Minh. Move as unobtrusively as possible through the bush on foot. The Bayard Group will be awaiting you at Kilometre 28.'

Colonel Charton obeyed the first part but a few minutes after the 3rd Battalion of the 3rd REI and the rest of the garrison had left Cao Bang strongpoint it blew up. Marching to meet them, the Bayard Group was already in difficulties, and their attack on the post at Dong Khe (which had fallen to a Viet Minh group after a two-day siege) failed, with the enemy splitting the column into small groups with the intention of annihilating them. The 1st BEP under the command of Major Segrétain formed the rearguard but was forced to withdraw in the face of overwhelming numbers. The remaining troops of the Bayard Group under the command of Colonel Lepage were now trapped in the Coc Xa gorge, with the 1st BEP above them. In the confusion, Lepage ordered the 1st BEP down into the valley, which involved a nightmare descent down a mountain path three feet (one metre) wide. On one side there was a rock face, on the other a 325-foot (100 metre) sheer drop down into the gorge. Viet Minh lurked everywhere. The Legion wounded were killed as they passed by on stretchers, and in the darkness others were dragged over the edge by suicidal guerrillas. One hundred legionnaires died on this descent, and of a group of trainee NCOs at the top of the cliff only seven survived.

Next morning Colonel Lepage decided on a desperate plan to break out to rejoin Charton's column. Major Segrétain's request to do it in daytime was refused, and although his remaining 210 legionnaires were in position by midnight on 7 October, it was dawn before he was ordered to attack, the delay resulting from the need to regroup the survivors of the Bayard Group. Too late for surprise and too early for air support, the result was execution. Men fell and dragged themselves up again, the wounded fighting from the ground whilst those unfortunate enough to be taken prisoner were clubbed to death by the Viet Minh. Others committed suicide. In minutes 120 legionnaires had died. The break-out was made by Moroccans of the *8e Tirailleurs Marocains* who rushed forward, foam on their lips, mad with fear, through the Viet Minh towards Charton's column about a mile (less than two kilometres) away.

Colonel Charton, his legionnaires, and the Moroccan troops had left Cao Bang in good order despite the 2,000 civilian refugees accompanying them. Upon receiving news of the Bayard Group's débâcle at Coc Xa gorge, he had the equipment destroyed and moved to assist, the legionnaires hacking through the vegetation at 1,000 yards (925 metres) an hour. Closing with the battle, they heard the sound of firing, the legionnaires responding to the order 'Faster!' in their endeavours to help their comrades. Pressing back the Viet Minh, the column broke through on the morning of 8 October to a position above Coc Xa.

At about 09.00, Colonel Charton saw the Moroccans coming and, although the legionnaires of the 3rd Battalion of the 3rd REI held off enemy attacks, there was chaos in the rear as Charton's Moroccans panicked. 'Who's in command of this rabble?' yelled the Colonel. There was no reply. The officers of the *8e Tirailleurs Marocains* had torn off their rank badges, and Lepage was in tears. Charton, realizing the end had come, went off to fight to the end as an infantryman, alongside the remaining legionnaires. After being wounded three times, he and three legionnaires were taken prisoner. The remainder of the 3rd Battalion of the 3rd REI and the 1st BEP had vanished, only three survivors reaching That Khe shortly before it was taken by Giap's men. Captain (later Lieutenant-Colonel) Pierre Jeanpierre fought in this battle, and he and a few of his men managed to extricate themselves and after great hardships reached Lang Son, a modern European-style city with 100,000 inhabitants.

It was expected that the French would make a stand here but headquarters at Hanoi had instructed Colonel Constans to evacuate Lang Son without a fight, an order the Viet Minh found hard to believe although they were delighted to capture thirteen heavy guns, 125 mortars, forty-five vehicles, three armoured cars and 940 machine-guns.

In retrospect, it was the loss of Dong Khe, control of the RC4 and the Cao Bang ridge which caused the French to lose their hold on the country. It gave the enemy a large area of difficult country alongside the Chinese frontier, enough military hardware to equip a division, and it cost the French 6,000 casualties. To the Legion it meant the loss of the 1st BEP, the third battalion of the 3rd REI and a large part of the 2nd Battalion of the 3rd REI. Something had to be done in the face of this catastrophe and in December 1950 General de Lattre arrived to take command of the military and political administration. After reviewing the situation, he had a large number of concrete forts constructed around the Red River delta, naming the resulting network of fortifications the de Lattre Line. Amongst the troops stationed there were units of the 2nd REI, 5th REI and the 13th DBLE. De Lattre's plan succeeded in halting three attempts in 1951 by the Viet Minh to move towards conventional warfare which brought about an improvement in French morale. After the battles at Vinh Yen, Mao Khe and Day River, General de Lattre launched a major attack on Hoa Binh, the Legion contributing the 1st BEP, 2nd BEP and the 2nd and 3rd Battalions of the 13th DBLE to the attacking force.

Unfortunately, increasing pressure from the Viet Minh led to a costly abandonment by the French in February 1952. In October of that year the Ngia Lo Ridge was lost to the Viet Minh and General Salan (who had replaced an ill de Lattre towards the end of 1951) launched 'Operation Lorraine' to cross the Viet Minh rear as they moved southwards after the Ngia Lo Ridge battles. Involving 30,000 men, the thrust penetrated some 100 miles (160 kilometres) into what was Viet Minh territory, but in the end the French had to conduct a fighting withdrawal as they retired to the Delta. Admiral Arthur W. Radford, Chief of Staff of the American Combined Forces, was to express the view at the time of the battle of Dien Bien Phu that the French 'lost the Indo-Chinese War in 1952 when General Salan failed to reoccupy Lai Kay'. General Giap's attack on the isolated French base at Na San in the Black River valley was repulsed, costing him one of his regular divisions but encouraging French planners to the opinion that isolated 'airheads' had a certain invincibility. Any success was welcome, but wrong conclusions were drawn and inexorably led to the final battle at Dien Bien Phu.

The Legion's German battalion's successful attacks on the Ho Chi Minh trail (Red Highway) and associated guerrilla bases had put the fate of the 'liberation' movement at stake. Viet Minh terrorists were supplied by means of this incredible network of trails, a twelve-foot (3.6 metre) wide road through the jungle which for many years had been suspected but never proven. It was a

Legionnaires in the foyer at Sidi-bel-Abbès, February 1951

The colour of the Legion is paraded in Alsace, December 1944

Admiral Jean de Laborde salutes Lieutenant-Colonel Magrin-Vernerey
(later Monclar) as he embarks with a detachment of the Legion (13th
DBLE) at Brest in April 1940, prior to sailing to Norway

The colour of the Legion is decorated by General de Gaulle, Nice, April
1945

The 1st REC under training in Morocco during World War II

Monument to the dead of the Legion at the Quartier Viénot, Sidi-bel-
Abbès, 1946

A Legion mortar post at Cao Bang, 1950

A legionnaire of the Compagnie de Réparation Elémentaire, repairing AFVs at Dien Bien Phu

Legionnaires of the 1st Battalion of the 2nd REI make their way through a
paddy field in Indo-China, October 1953

The colour and the colour party of the 1st CSPL, parading at the Fête de Camerone, Fort Flatters, 30 April 1958

An AML M8 of the CSPLE in January 1957 on patrol in the region of Ouled-Rabak (southern Algeria)

A section of AMX 13 tanks of the 2nd Squadron of the 2nd REC pass through Fort Fouad during the Suez operation, November 1956

Le Boedj de Tabelbala, Sahara base of the 'compagnie porte' of the 2nd REI, 1966

Legionnaires leap from a Boeing-Vertol H-21 'Shawnee' helicopter –
nicknamed the 'flying banana'. The first of these arrived in Algeria in
1957. Each could carry twenty men – two complete infantry sections

Winter operations in Algeria, 1961

masterpiece of camouflage: at less densely wooded sections, trees had been roped together overhead to provide unbroken cover. A similar arrangement existed in open ravines, where wire netting supported the creepers, and difficult sections were 'paved' with gravel or logs. There were checkpoints, rest houses and service stations for the maintenance of carts and bicycles. Observation posts were sited throughout the area to warn of aircraft and possible troop movements.

The international Communist media denounced the French use of Germans, accusing them of the massacre of innocent civilians and other crimes. In 1952 the Chamber of Deputies in Paris did what the Viet Minh could not achieve in five years and succumbed in five weeks to the pressure of this well-orchestrated campaign. 'Time-served' legionnaires resigned; the remainder were incorporated into other Legion units. By contrast the demand for manpower was so great that the Legion was obliged to reduce its training period, using raw recruits to replace these hardened veterans.

By 1953 the French had a new commander-in-chief, General Navarre, whose strategy was to launch minor thrusts against Giap whilst building up a strong reserve for a decisive battle in 1955, in order successfully to conclude this long-drawn-out struggle. Not only French forces were to be involved: an important contribution was to be made by the Vietnamese National Army, rapidly developing with the support of advisers and aid provided from the USA.

Navarre did, however, launch one major offensive. Code-named 'Operation Hirondelle', it took place in July 1953 and involved three parachute battalions, including the 2nd BEP. They successfully attacked Viet Minh bases around Lang Son at the same time as a large-scale amphibious operation took place in the waist of Annam. Their withdrawal by sea was covered by the 5th REI. During the following month the Na San garrison (who had repulsed Giap's forces the previous year) was successfully withdrawn, giving further support to the confidence which had evolved in isolated airheads.

Arising from this, and from his anticipation of an invasion of Laos, Navarre decided to establish a major airhead in the border hills by means of an airborne operation code named 'Operation Castor'. Accordingly, during November 1953 paras of the 1st BEP were dropped into the valley of Dien Bien Phu where the Legion

constructed a major fortress considered a natural bastion by the
French planners and situated some 200 miles north of Hanoi. The
chosen position was in a bowl of hills and was totally reliant on
supply by air. By March 1954 some 16,000 men formed the
garrison, and of these the first and second battalions of the 3rd REI,
the second and third battalions of the 13th DBLE and the 1st BEP
was the Legion's contribution of 5,000 men at the outset. There was
an Algerian regiment, four French paratroop battalions, two Thai
battalions and one Moroccan battalion. General Cogny, although
based at Hanoi, was the general in command of Dien Bien Phu
where the forces came under the local command of a cavalry officer,
Colonel (later General) Christian de Castries, with Lieutenant-
Colonel Jules Gaucher in command of the Legion units, which held
the key positions. Lengthening of the airstrip and construction of an
associated series of strongpoints had been undertaken by the
Legion. When René Pleven, the French minister of the Armed
Forces, toured the camp and nearly fell through a dug-out roof, he
commented to Gaucher, 'Colonel, isn't it true, unfortunately, that
we have to reckon with the Viet artillery, since I gather they have
some?' To which Gaucher replied, 'Monsieur le Ministre, we shall
fight as at Verdun'. At no time in the Legion's history were
François Negrier's words, 'You legionnaires are soldiers in order to
die and I am sending you where you can die' more appropriate.

It was obvious that an attack was imminent and late in the
afternoon of 13 March 1954 Viet Minh troops attacked legionnaires
of the 13th DBLE on one of the strong points codenamed 'Béatrice'.
Such was the ferocity of that attack that within a matter of hours, a
Legion battalion was destroyed, Lieutenant-Colonel Gaucher,
Major Pegeaux (commander of the 3rd Battalion of the 13th
DBLE) and four officers were killed, one wounded, nearly 400 men
killed, missing or wounded. Gaucher's place was taken by
Lieutenant-Colonel Maurice Lemeunier, who volunteered to take
this command and arrived, it is said, at Dien Bien Phu in a
helicopter bearing red cross markings. The struggle continued with
the Viet Minh battering one hill strongpoint after another,
following up their artillery barrages with infantry attacks. On 30
March 1954, counter-attacking legionnaires of the 2nd REI forced
Giap's men back, recapturing the strong point at Élaine 2 to the
south-east of Dien Bien Phu, but he had won the strategic heights
to the north and north-east, enabling him to systematically destroy

the remainder of the French garrison at the same time as the Paris radio announced 'At Dien Bien Phu, the situation is well under control'. Within three days it was virtually impossible to supply the base from the air and it was clear to the defenders that there could only be one outcome to the battle unless some miraculous event occurred. This might have occurred if Navarre or Cogny had gone to Dien Bien Phu and taken command from the sorely tried cavalryman, de Castries. It was not a question of courage, but other responsibilities and a personal conflict of opinion between the two generals which prevented such an occurrence. Despite its official statements, the French government recognized that the war was going badly and on 25 March 1954, the chief of the French Armed Forces went to Washington to seek American aid. The US Army's G3 Planning Division concluded that nuclear weapons could be used to attack Viet Minh forces and their bases. Meanwhile, the epic battle continued. It was to last fifty-seven days, throughout which Genèvieve de Galard, an air nurse, worked in the underground hospital and infirmary, joining the Ouled Naïls (the North African prostitutes from the BMC) who moved silently between the dead and dying as they assisted the medical staff. She had arrived on a Dakota which had engine trouble and was destroyed on the ground by the Viet Minh, who used their artillery to prevent the French using the airstrip from the end of March, preventing the evacuation of the wounded and bringing about major problems of supply.

Meanwhile the planners in Washington presented another study on 8 April proposing that from one to six 31-kiloton bombs be dropped from carrier-based aircraft. Each bomb had an explosive power approximately three times as great as the bomb dropped on Hiroshima. However, the plan met with bitter opposition from General Matthew Ridgeway, the US Army Chief of Staff and the US Intelligence and the Air Force considered that the terrain around Dien Bien Phu would reduce the effectiveness of a nuclear attack or a saturation attack with conventional weapons. The next stage was a study of the possible consequences of US intervention using air and sea power and it was concluded that this would lead to a commitment of ground forces with a distinct possibility of Chinese retaliation.

As the situation worsened, it was decided to reinforce the garrison and on 10 April 1954 a force of 3,000 paras made a heroic combat drop. Amongst them were 700 legionnaires of the 2nd BEP, together with volunteers from the 3rd REI, who made this drop without parachute training. They had no more injuries than sustained by the regular paras who dropped with them thereby revising military thinking on airborne operations. These drops of trained and untrained paras were to continue nightly when the weather conditions were right, often with small numbers until on the night of 6/7 May the five Dakotas with the final hundred reinforcements turned back as they approached Dien Bien Phu, due to the inability of the pilots to identify the small dropping zone.

Besides the military offensive, the Viet Minh developed their psychological warfare with incessant tannoy appeals to the defenders, 'Why be a slave of the colonialists?' 'Uncle Ho offers you life and freedom'. On Camerone Day (30 April 1954) the approach was varied: 'Why continue to fight?' 'Why do what the legionnaires did at Camerone – get themselves massacred?' Many North Africans and Thais laid down their arms, but when Lieutenant-Colonel Lemeunier read the whole camp the Camerone story over the tannoy, more than 1,000 men sang *Le Boudin* and drowned out the Viet Minh propaganda. Would it have helped if the Americans had intervened? Admiral Radford, the Chairman of the Joint Chiefs-of-Staff argued successfully that any gain from effective intervention would be counter-productive in relation to the liability it would incur, but politicians were viewing the war in terms of advantage to the US and the free world if the Communists could be defeated.

The end was near on 6 May, with only a fragment of the base still under French control, and although a break-out was considered by Colonel de Castries, it would have resulted in a massacre of the wounded. The next day the base fell to the Viet Minh, and although a few escaped, some 7,000 troops including legionnaires shambled into humiliation and captivity. To General Giap, who had thrown into the battle 50,000 infantry, supported by 200 guns and anti-aircraft weapons, the cost had been 22,000 casualties. But what did it matter? The hated French had been beaten despite conducting one of the epic defences of military history.

On 8 May 1954, news of the fall of Dien Bien Phu was brought to the recruits and veterans by Colonel Paul Gardy, parading on the square of the Quartier Viénot in Sidi-bel-Abbès.

'Dien Bien Phu has just been taken. We are assembled here to do homage to the sacrifice of those who have fallen in this epic struggle. We shall now present arms to the colours which have vanished in battle.'

There was a short silence, and then he called the roll:

'The 2nd and 3rd Battalions of the 13th DBLE.'

'The 2nd and 3rd Battalions of the 3rd REI.'

'The 1st Battalion of the 2nd REI.'

'The 1st and 2nd Parachute Battalions.'

Another silence and the 'last post' sounded. The Legion was united in its agony that had brought such losses causing it to exist only in rear bases and establishment figures, for in addition to the larger groupings, the fallen had included the 3rd REI personnel of the 1st Mixed Mortar Company (1er CMMLE); volunteers from the 3rd REI and the 2nd BEP who parachuted into Dien Bien Phu without para training and legionnaires from the 5th REI which provided the garrison's 2nd Mixed Mortar Company (2e CMMLE). The 2nd BEP was reformed shortly after the defeat by re-numbering the 3rd BEP, which landed at Haiphong in May 1954.

France had lost the struggle for Indo-China, and the new Mendès-France Government had to make peace with Ho Chi Minh. Metropolitan France was in turmoil, and there was much effort in trying to apportion the blame. Who was to be the scapegoat? The Legion, the Algerians, the Moroccans or the Thais? For how many French soldiers had fought at Dien Bien Phu in the name of French colonial policy? Of the total French casualty bill of 22,000, the Legion had suffered 10,483 dead.

Out of the 6,328 legionnaires captured during the war in Indo-China, only 2,567 returned alive, the last sixteen not until 1959 – and they were paid for! Legion units remained in Indo-China whilst negotiations took place in Geneva which resulted in an armistice on 30 August 1954, leaving Ho Chi Minh controlling the north from Hanoi and a temporary administration controlling the south, with its headquarters at Saigon. Prisoners returning from Indo-China had to be re-assimilated into the Legion. Many had changed character, adopting the habits of reflection and self-criticism which made them difficult to control. To overcome the problem and re-instill into them the spirit of the

Legion, the returning troops were remustered into units consisting of older legionnaires and new recruits; their officers were promoted and new men took their place.

It was time for a re-think, a turning-point, and the French High Command reduced the strength from 30,000 to 13,000 legionnaires. Re-engagements were discouraged, and recruiting became selective, although Vietnamese who returned to Algeria with the Legion were formed into auxiliary units which fought alongside their adoptive regiments.

Despite the reservations of the military planners, it was to be the turn of the Americans. They had no more chance of winning the minds of the people than the French, nor of beating the Viet Minh, for whom there could only be one policy – bomb for bomb, bullet for bullet, murder for murder. Unfortunately, the lessons had not been learned. There was a certain smug arrogance. The outcome was inevitable, although no one could, or would, believe it at that time.

6. The Algerian War

It was 'business as usual' in Morocco for the small number of legionnaires from the 4th REI who had remained there, although the regiment itself had been disbanded on 14 November 1940, as a result of supplying men for the 11th and 12th REs and later the 13th DBLE. On 16 May 1946 the 4th Foreign Legion half-brigade of Morocco (4th DBLE) was formed for garrison and police duties. A similar unit – but without the suffix 'of Morocco' – had been established on 20 August 1941 and adopted the regimental colour of the 4th REI, first established in Senegal, later serving in Tunisia, before being incorporated in the 1st Foreign Marching Infantry Regiment (1st REIM) which was itself disbanded on 3 June 1943.

Whilst there had been a few incidents during the war years, the riots which broke out in Setif during the 'Victory in Europe Day' celebrations on 8 May 1945 were a foretaste of future problems. Exception was taken to the marchers carrying the green-and-white flag of Abd-el-Kader, shots were fired, and so began a massacre which caused the deaths of 103 Europeans with more than a hundred wounded. The Jihad (Holy War) as it was viewed by the mob, spread to other towns before the army could restore order, which resulted in some 6,000 Muslims being killed in reprisals.

The re-formed 4th DBLE based one battalion at Fez, another at Meknes, with a 'mounted company' at Ksar-es-Souk, but in June 1947 the 4th Battalion was sent to Madagascar to restore order.

Despite the influx of new recruits into the Legion, the need for trained legionnaires in other areas of activities resulted in a continued drain of the 4th DBLE's manpower, further accentuated when, in October 1947, one company from each battalion was used to establish the new 2nd BEP, and one year later, on 16 October 1948, the regiment resumed the title as the 4th REI. Further depletion of its strength occurred when the 3rd Battalion was sent to Tonkin as part of the 5th REI, which was re-formed in July 1949. Still further reductions took place, and by the end of 1951 only one battalion remained, based at Meknes, although the regiment's presence in Morocco was strengthened in the December by the return of the 4th Battalion, which was based at Fez, although it performed an autonomous role.

The aspirations for independence in Morocco started to surface again, and in April 1952 there was anti-French rioting which involved the Legion in continuous police action throughout the remainder of the French protectorate, which lasted until 1957, when independence was granted and the Legion left Morocco. In addition to the 4th REI, an independent group of motorized companies also served in Morocco. This had been formed and based at Agadir and in 1945 was named the Motorized Group of the Foreign Legion, Morocco (GPLEM). A reorganization in the mid-1950s resulted in the two battalions of the 4th REI and the GPLEM being made into the one regiment. Other mobile support was provided by the 2nd REC, which was reduced to three squadrons by 1955, when it absorbed the 2nd Amphibious Group of the 1st REC upon its return from Vietnam.

Whilst the French authorities had time to take the measure of the Communist aspirations in Vietnam (but not, as it turned out, the political will or perhaps the economic power to control them), they were very nervous about the political situation in North Africa, which economically and politically meant more to them. Legionnaires were considered to be reliable in comparison with the troops recruited from ethnic communities, who, it was thought, might well side with their countrymen if any rebellion should show signs of being successful. However, the varied backgrounds of legionnaires also concerned the authorities, and whilst it was permissible to sing '*Deutschland über Alles*' in the barracks, a similar rendering of the '*Internationale*', or 'Red Flag' was forbidden, and it was a serious offence to bring into barracks copies of the local Communist papers. This nervousness communicated itself to the legionnaires, and those about whom there was the slightest doubt in regard to their connections or political ideas were posted, immediately on completion of their basic training, to Vietnam where, paradoxically, France was fighting a bitter war with a known Communist adversary.

*

That the 'Legion is our homeland' was never more clearly demonstrated than during the fighting and in the emotive issues which surrounded the Algerian war, which lasted from 1954 until 1962. The war cost the Legion sixty-five officers, 278 NCOs and 1,633 legionnaires dead and almost brought about the Legion's disbandment; it set Frenchman against Frenchman, even taking the struggle to the streets of Paris.

It was a British legionnaire known as Jean Marsal who alerted the Legion to the scale of the preparations being made for the forthcoming rebellion in Algeria. Working under cover for the Legion, he passed on much valuable information before he was murdered and his body thrown into the harbour at Algiers. In April 1954 the various liberation movements had formed a new body called the Revolutionary Committee of United Action (CRUA) and, by a historic chance, its first full meeting took place on the day Dien Bien Phu fell. It gave a tremendous boost to the revolutionaries, and on 10 October the new movement not only fixed its name – the National Liberation Federation (FLN) but also decided the date for the start of the revolt throughout Algeria – All Saints' Day (*Le Toussaint*), 1 November 1954. In the early hours groups of rebels – *fellagha*, known to the French as '*fells*' – attacked several targets in Constantine province, including a police station and a bus, in which they killed a French schoolteacher, Guy Monnerot, and a French reserve officer who tried to save him. At first the French, not unreasonably, did not give much importance to the incidents, dealing with the situation in the traditional manner by sending a half *bataillon de marche*, this time from the 1st RE, to sort out the problem.

However, intelligence officers were beginning to learn more of their opponents, and that an organization known as the National Liberation Federation (FLN) had been formed with a military wing, Algerian National Liberation Army (ALN), with the objective of expelling the French from Algeria. This was not a hit-and-run affair but a well-planned organization which had divided the country into six *wilayas* (military districts) and *katibas* (companies) which consisted of about 150 to 186 *fellagha*. Although in the early days of the war the rebels were able to present a semblance of military organization, this never developed, and the struggle consisted of a succession of encounters with small armed bands, seldom larger than a *katiba*. For their part, the French involved 400,000 of their troops, of whom the Legion maintained a strength of about 20,000 men.

At this time overall control of the Legion was vested in the Legion's Autonomous Group (GALE), which had been established in 1950. The 1st RE provided depot services and training at its bases in Sidi-bel-Abbès, Saida and Mascara, with other units based throughout North Africa, to which the legionnaires were posted as they returned from Vietnam.

In January 1955 the original half *bataillon de marche* was relieved by a full *bataillon de marche* which in July became the third company of the 3rd REI, which was disbanded in September 1957. It was from this company that the first two legionnaires died for France in Algeria: Kreuze and Zelli, who were killed on 18 March 1955. The evolving pattern of the Algerian war brought about a need for mobile units to deal with the *fellagha*, and this was met early in 1955 by the formation at Ain-Sefra of the Motorized Group of the Foreign Legion, Algeria, (GPLE d'Algérie) from the 4th Company of the 1st RE, which became the 21st, 22nd, 23rd and 24th Motorized Companies, the latter forming the nucleus of the 4th CPSL formed in January 1956. The CPSLs were long-range desert patrol groups principally involved in the security of remote outposts, highways and the oil-rich sands of the Sahara.

Paratroops were to play an important part in this war, and the first to be involved were from the 2nd REP which had been formed in December 1955 (after landing at Mers-el-Kebir in November 1955 as the 2nd BEP) and absorbing in Indo-China the personnel of the 3rd BEP which had been raised in Algeria during the previous August. Whilst there had been several attempts by the FLN to exclude women and children from their attacks, a change of policy in June 1955 declared war on all French civilians. The upshot was the Philippeville massacre, which occurred on 20 August 1955 and which caused the deaths in the most brutal manner of seventy-one Europeans and fifty-two pro-French Arabs, while several thousand Muslims died in the backlash. From a series of incidents, a war to the death had begun. Did anyone recall the words of Baron Lacuée written in 1831 as the Legion arrived in the Magrheb? 'As long as you keep Algiers, you will constantly be at war with Africa, sometimes the war will seem to end; but those people will not hate you any the less; it will be a half-extinguished fire that will smoulder under the ash and which, at the first opportunity, will burst into a vast conflagration.'

However, there was another side of the wave of Arab nationalism which involved Egypt and caused French and British relations with Egypt to deteriorate. On 7 September the 10th Parachute Division, which included the 1st REP, had arrived in Cyprus from Algeria as part of the Anglo-French military build-up in connection with the political situation in the Middle East, arising from the Egyptian Government's surprise occupation and nationalization of the Suez Canal on 26 July 1956. A month later Lieutenant-Colonel Gamal Abdel Nasser became President. Whilst the action undoubtedly angered the French, it is more probable that the Egyptian attitude to what it described as 'imperialist colonialists' and the encouragement and material help the Egyptian Government was going to give to the FLN had the stronger influence on French policy. Not only were the Egyptians broadcasting anti-French and anti-British propaganda throughout Africa but Lieutenant-Colonel Nasser, King Saud of Saudi Arabia and President Kuwalty of Syria issued a joint appeal calling for 'drastic action' against France in Algeria. Nasser had been fanning the flames throughout the Arab world, whipping up nationalistic revolutionary fever through Egyptian propaganda broadcasts from a radio station in Cairo known as 'The Voice of Africa'. This statement was interpreted as indicating the possibility of Egyptian – or other – volunteers participating in the Algerian war, or even a full-scale military adventure. Had the French known of the fighting ability of the Egyptian army, they might have not been quite so concerned, from a military standpoint, for the Egyptians, attacked by the Israelis on 29 October, were quickly destroyed, giving Israel control of the Sinai peninsula by 2 November in a brief but brilliant campaign.

The situation had been inflamed by an Anglo-French ultimatum to the Egyptian and Israeli Governments which, besides calling for a cessation of the fighting, also demanded that the Egyptian Government agree to Anglo-French forces moving into key positions at Port Said, Ismailia and Suez in order to guarantee freedom of transit through the Suez Canal. The ultimatum continued by requiring acceptance within twelve hours, after which British and French forces would intervene to ensure compliance. The Israelis accepted, because they had been participants in the plot from the beginning, the Egyptians did not, so after air attacks on 31 October, 1 and 2 November by British and French aircraft,

Anglo-French paratroops landed at Port Said on 5 November, followed by a British amphibious squadron of tanks. By the evening of that day Port Said was occupied, and on the following day seaborne reinforcements arrived, including the 1st REP and the 2nd Squadron of the 2nd REC, with AMX 13 tanks, who landed without opposition at Port Fuad (to the east of Port Said) at 05.35 hours. However, at 06.15 hours, in a short, sharp battle for possession of a police post, two legionnaires were killed. At midnight a ceasefire came into effect, but Anglo-French forces remained in the area of the Suez Canal until withdrawing on 22 December, when they marched past their commanders with colours flying and in full battle order before embarking on their transport at Port Fuad, which, in the case of the legionnaires, returned them to Algeria and their barracks at Zeralda.

In Algeria the tactics of the ALN followed a similar pattern to Vietnam in that they brought terror to isolated communities, looting and destroying, killing and butchering pro-French Arabs and village chiefs in front of their families. Not unnaturally the terrified villagers gave no information to the Legion patrols, and in an effort to bring about a measure of control, the French mounted a vast census operation, issuing every man, woman and child in Algeria with an identity card. To make matters harder for the *fellagha*, the Moroccan and Tunisian frontiers (from which countries it will be recalled the Legion had withdrawn) were sealed by electrified wire fences stretching some 200 miles (320 kilometres). That along the Tunisian frontier was known as the 'Guelma Line' and that along the Moroccan frontier as the 'Morice Line'. The barricades were erected approximately a mile (1.6 kilometres) inside the frontiers, leaving a 'no-man's land' in between, where both French and Arabs mounted patrols and ambushes. However, the barricades were not impregnable. The *fellagha* used bangalore torpedoes which, filled with explosives, fed under the wire and detonated, blew a hole in the wire and exploded any mines in the vicinity, enabling the *fellagha* to pass through the wire. The Morice Line had blockhouses at regular intervals, and the electrified wire was supported by minefields, searchlights and regular patrols by the Legion, the inhospitable desert to the south being patrolled by the 2nd REC, which became involved in Algeria in 1957 principally in the south, although it spent a period between 1959 and 1960 in the central zone.

The defensive lines were, however, effective, and besides being designed to kill had electronic devices which quickly pinpointed breakthroughs, enabling the mobile units to track down the infiltrators rapidly. Helicopters were used for surveillance and, try as they would, the ALN could not overcome the defences. As they escalated their attacks, their losses increased at a greater rate in the face of constantly improving French defensive tactics.

Most of the skirmishes took place in the Tunisian frontier zone, and after the 4th REI arrived from Morocco in April 1957 it first served in the area between Bône and Tebessa, then in the Aurès and Nementchas, before it was transferred in June 1959 to the Guelma region to cover the Tunisian border defences, a duty it performed until early 1962. After having served in both south-east and central Algeria, the 1st REC undertook patrol duty in the Tunisian frontier zone until 1959, when it became involved in operations in the Aurès, Nementchas and south Constantine, often fighting as helicopter-borne infantry. From 1956 the domain of the 3rd REI was in the triangle of the Collo-Djidjelli peninsula, whilst the 2nd REI, after returning from Morocco, took up positions in eastern Algeria in the areas of Bône and Djidjelli, where it became a motorized regiment. The 1st and 3rd Companies were disbanded and the 2nd Company formed the basis of a new GCP 1 which had three companies and went into action in October 1956. In the same month, the GCPLE d'Algérie was disbanded and re-formed as the GCP 2, also with three companies, moving in March 1957 to Ain-Sefra where it joined GCP 1. For the next five years the two formations were involved in operations in south-west Algeria, in particular patrolling the Morice Line. Towns and villages were garrisoned by French troops, many of them national service conscripts serving for two years, whereas the Legion and the regular paratroops patrolled and fought the rebels in the Aurès and Kabylia mountains.

Although the Oran province remained relatively calm, patrol and surveillance duties were carried out in north-west Algeria from early in 1956 until October 1958 by the 5th REI which was based at Arzew on the coast to the west of Oran.

However, the administrative system in Algeria brought problems for the security forces insofar as *fellagha* caught by the army had to be handed over to the police. This was not the Legion's way of dealing with such matters, and legionnaires became very embittered when captured rebels were released and back in action. In the Legion's view, they were defending their homeland in a struggle which appeared to have no end, as Governments in Paris sought a political solution which would maintain a French presence in Algeria, the very opposite to the rebels' cause.

But the Legion itself had changed and through its bitter experiences in Vietnam had not only learned new tactical skills but had developed new units to exploit them – in particular, the paratroops. After returning from the Anglo-French Suez operation, the 1st REP came under the command of Lieutenant-Colonel Pierre Jeanpierre, in March 1957. The regiment had suffered grievous losses in Vietnam but was rejuvenated with carefully selected officers and men and based at Zeralda, twelve miles (20 kilometres) west of Algiers. Acting mainly as a mobile reserve, the 1st REP was to achieve extraordinary success, particularly on operations in wild, mountainous countryside, where the legionnaires accepted the discomfiture of the terrain, using the cover of the scrub to greater advantage than did the *fellagha*! It was here that the 1st REP virtually destroyed the ALN, who changed their tactics by moving into the towns and planting bombs in public places with devastating effect, as part of a campaign of terror.

To deal with this development, the French Commander-in-Chief, General Raoul Salan, instructed the commander of the 10th Parachute Division, General Jacques Massu, to move into Algiers and solve the problem, including the removal of two particular FLN terrorists, Yacef Saadi and Ali la Pointe, the masterminds behind the bombing in Algiers, which was particularly severe at the end of January 1957. Immediately a barbed-wire barricade was thrown around the Casbah, but although the intensive searches and interrogations soon quietened matters down, Yacef Saadi and Ali la Pointe managed to evade capture until 24 September, Saadi being captured in a skilful undercover operation in which Legion Adjutant Laszlo Tasnady had the initial breakthrough when disguised as an Arab woman. Ali la Pointe died two weeks later, on 8 October, evading arrest in a house in the Casbah.

It was during an action in the Guelma area in April 1958, when a ALN command unit was directing some 1,000 men in attacks against towns and villages, that the 1st REP under the command of Lieutenant-Colonel Pierre Jeanpierre developed the tactics which enabled the legionnaires quickly to destroy the *fellagha*, without great cost in casualties to the Legion.

The first essential was to act only on precise information, and then, upon locating the *fellagha*, helicopters would land one company which would engage the enemy fire whilst a second company would advance in line abreast. Upon receiving a signal, the legionnaires halted, hurling grenades, then hurled another salvo of grenades at the enemy, the procedure continuing until the ground had been quartered. Attacks commenced in the morning, concluded before nightfall and were supported by fighter aircraft rather than artillery. Legionnaires were equipped with machine-pistols and grenades, and the underlying principle was to swamp the area with maximum fire power, the legionnaires maintaining the momentum of the battle, which was controlled by Lieutenant-Colonel Jeanpierre from his command helicopter circling overhead.

Tragedy struck, however, on 29 May in the tangled scrub of Djebel Mermera, near Guelma, in the course of a similar action when Jeanpierre's helicopter was shot down and he was killed. Such was the angry reaction of the Legion that they did not stop fighting until the last *fellagha* on that hill had died or surrendered, and indeed it was the 1st REP that conducted the 'battle of Guelma' throughout 1958 and 1959. Lieutenant-Colonel Jeanpierre was one of the Legion's heroes. He was a pre-war legionnaire who had fought with the 6th REI in Eritrea and afterwards had chosen repatriation to France. There he had joined the French resistance and was captured and tortured by the Gestapo before being deported to Mauthaussen extermination camp, where he was one of the few survivors.

Jeanpierre's funeral, when 30,000 people turned out at El Alia, was a very emotive occasion, and his death did much to affect the course of the Algerian war. Lieutenant Roger Degueldre of the 1st REP, placing his hand on his former commanding officer's coffin, made the oath: 'Rather die, Colonel, than leave Algeria in the hands of the FLN.'

Between 1954 and the day Jeanpierre was buried, six French Governments had collapsed in their endeavours to deal with the Algerian crisis, the latest being that of Pierre Pflimlin, who resigned on 29 May 1958, having been invested as Prime Minister only on 14 May. Meanwhile, in Cairo the revolutionaries had proclaimed a provisional Government of the Algerian Revolution (GPRA). As a counter-balance, a Committee of Public Safety had been formed in 1958 by General Jacques Massu and the Gaullists, who prevailed upon Salan to send a message to the French President Coty: 'The responsible military authorities esteem it an imperative necessity to appeal to a national arbiter with a view to constituting a Government of Public Safety. A call for calm, by this higher authority, is alone capable of re-establishing the situation.'

All was confusion in Paris – there was no Government. Whilst de Gaulle was not mentioned, it was clear who was wanted, and indeed a direct appeal was sent to him. The view in Algeria was that it would remain French; there was an air of euphoria, and even Muslims joined the colonialists to chant '*Algérie Française!*' Now there was revolutionary fever in Paris, with plans being formulated in Algiers for military intervention in France to force the hand of the Government. The provisional date fixed for the operation, code-named 'Resurrection' was 27/28 May, and on 24 May Massu's paras seized power in Corsica. An ultimatum was sent to President Coty from Algiers and on 1 June 1958 de Gaulle assumed the Premiership of France as the country hovered on the brink of civil war. Three days later he was in Algeria, kneeling at the tomb of Jeanpierre and afterwards placating the army and the French colonists, who were dissatisfied with the handling of the Algerian war, telling them – '*Je vous ai compris – Algérie Française.*' ('I understand you – French Algeria.') As the Muslims were intent on expelling the French, whose colonialists were intent on retaining the *status quo*, there seemed little room for compromise.

The 2nd REP was also based at Guelma in eastern Algeria throughout the war and undertook duties similar to the 1st REP, insofar as it acted as a highly professional mobile reserve on operations principally in the Guelma area, with particular reference to actions involving the Tunisian electrified barricade known as the Guelma Line. The 2nd REP, as part of the 25th Parachute Division, had conducted operations in the Kabylia mountains and the Aurès mountains and the Nementcha massif, often at heights of up to 7,000 feet (2,128 metres). Here the land was totally barren, with not a sign of vegetation, animal or bird life. The steep-sided valleys and gorges, however, were often covered in thick

Legionnaires at their leisure and on parade. *Left:* The Fête de Camerone, Indo-China 1952. Note the locally recruited legionnaire wearing a white beret instead of the kepi. *Right:* Belgian, Scottish and English legionnaires of the 1st Squadron of the 1st REC at Ferme Edelin-Albert, Algeria 1965. They are carrying 9mm MAT 49 sub-machine-guns. *Below:* Members of the 1st REC band at their headquarters, Camp Defile, in 1965. Behind is a line of EBRs.

Chad 1970: legionnaires in a
Transall aircraft prepare to jum

The 2nd REP on patrol in Algeria

The 2nd REP board their aircraft for a practice drop in Algeria, 1967

'Not every landing is a good one –
even in the 2nd REP'

A legionnaire of the 1st Battalion
of the 2nd REI in Indo-China, 30
October 1953

Legionnaires of the 1st RE firing .50 calibre Browning machine-guns.
These would normally be mounted on half-tracks

Legionnaires in Chad, 1970, about to board a helicopter

The colours of the 1st REC leaving Algeria on 22 October 1967 for the
Quartier Labouche, Orange, France

'Musique Principale de la Legion Etrangère' during the Fête de
Camerone, Aubagne, 30 April 1968

The 2nd REP loading equipment
at Solenzara for the emergency
mission to Zaire, 22 May 1978

VLRA of the 2nd REP on
reconnaissance in the Région de
Sountami (north of Ati), Chad,
February 1984

Kolwezi, May 1978: legionnaires of the 2nd REP evacuate wounded

Under the watchful eye of a legionnaire, PLO 'freedom fighters' move en
route to the docks at Beirut

The Fête de Camerone, 1986: former British legionnaires parade at the statue of Marshal Foch in London

A plaque identifying the squadron lines of the 1st Squadron of the 1st REC at Bous-Fer, 1965

undergrowth, which offered excellent cover for the *fellagha*. In winter it was freezing cold, wet and very windy, so that the legionnaires were in a constant state of discomfort. Besides personal weapons and kit, each man carried six days' ammunition and rations and half a two-man tent which was shared with a comrade.

Arising from the success of the mobile units, a major reorganization took place in October 1958, when the 3rd and 5th REIs were reorganized as intervention regiments to go in hot pursuit of the enemy. Each had two headquarters companies controlling two groups of four companies each. The 13th DBLE, which had always been considered a mountain unit, had been involved in operations along the Tunisian border and on the Nementcha massif. Reorganization in 1958 as an intervention unit resulted in the 13th DBLE being based at Batna and then Bougie.

A major change in the conduct of the war occurred when Air Force General Maurice Challe succeeded General Salan in December 1958. He devised a series of measures which became known as the 'Challe Plan', implemented early in 1959 as a major act of pacification. The villagers were moved from their homes into camps and whilst this made protection of the population easier, it reduced French prestige, at the same time assisting recruitment for the FLN. However, Challe's methods worked and, using tactics described earlier in the chapter, the 1st REP now spearheaded the hunt for the armed bands.

Sudden death was a permanent possibility, and in the Nementchas, a staff sergeant of the 1st REP was knifed in the street, with the result that his company descended on the Arab quarter, and fifteen minutes later sixty-four Arabs were dead, killed by automatic fire or bayonet. The Legion began to feel a stranger in a country which it considered its own, insofar as it was the young conscripts of the French army who had the pleasure of the permanent camps and garrisoned the towns and villages, whereas the Legion was invariably quartered outside the barbed wire surrounding a town. They were not welcomed by the Arabs, who shut their shops, or by the Europeans, who raised their prices. This is probably one of the reasons for the Legion taking its mess, cinema and brothel with it on active service.

The Algerian war, with its inconclusive skirmishes and apparent lack of cohesion, reduced the morale of the Legion, which sought positive action. It was not a popular struggle in any way; it did not attract anyone, and the Legion had a problem in attracting recruits when, of necessity, the Government's policy of reducing its strength in the aftermath of the Vietnam war had to be reversed. In fact, in 1955 the recruitment was 2,981 compared with 5,447 in 1954 and 6,327 in 1953. So serious was the situation that re-engagements were rare, and between September 1955 and July 1956 not a single legionnaire of the 13th DBLE applied for re-engagement. Pay, because it was in their own country on peacetime duty, was down to 190 francs per month; medals were rare because the actions were undertaken technically in 'Metropolitan France', and living-conditions in the temporary camps were poor. Whilst conditions were generally better for the paratroops in regard to living-quarters and pay, the hard fighting in 1956 alone cost the 1st REP one third of its strength of 1,200 killed and wounded in the three months of fighting.

Something had to be done, and as always the legionnaires rose to the occasion, with the 13th DBLE making its camp at Bougie a splendid establishment, with the result that morale rose, the legionnaires appreciating that they were able to return from operations and enjoy their comforts. There was a return to traditional ceremonials, with the guard in parade uniforms. The call '*Au Caid*' (salute to the commanding officer) which was particular to Legion units, was re-established. It is a unique ceremony: the call is sounded once a day when colours are in the camp, and the only recipient of it is the unit commander. As he arrives in the morning, the guard parades, each legionnaire calling out his name as he presents arms. In return, the commander salutes and inspects the guard, and simultaneously the whole camp comes to attention. These ceremonials are very important in fostering the *esprit de corps* of the Legion. For instance, lunch in the officers' mess is mandatory, with a number of formalities, including the singing of '*Le Boudin*' before the reading of the menu.

7 Independence

After General Challe's large-scale operations in 1959, the French never again encountered more than the remnants of armed groups, forced to revert to the pre-1955 terrorist methods. However, despite the military successes, the political solution took a different direction, and there was great dismay when General de Gaulle broadcast on 16 September 1959, outlining his alternatives for Algeria: independence, complete union with France or self-government under French rule. The broadcast was followed by a distinct change in the political attitude towards the war, which militarily the French were winning but at a cost which was endangering the French economy. Bearing in mind the cost, it is open to speculation as to how long the French could have maintained the *status quo* and proceeded to the stage where hostilities ceased in their favour.

His speech was greeted with dismay, and in discussions amongst the generals the seeds of insurrection were sown, creating great discontent in the army, particularly within the elite paratroop units. In January General Jacques Massu, Commander of the 10th Parachute Division, was unfortunate enough to make a number of indiscreet remarks to a West German journalist, in particular criticism of General de Gaulle, who promptly recalled Massu to Paris on 18 January, sacked him and sent him as Garrison Commander to Metz. On hearing the news, the French National Front formed on 1 November 1958 – *Le Toussaint* (All Saints' Day), the outbreak of the Algerian revolution on 1 November 1954 – declared that a general strike would commence on 24 January 1960, and by Saturday the 23rd their troops were massing. The 10th Parachute Division (now commanded by General Gracieux) was recalled from Kabylia, but it appears that General Challe was unaware of the extent of the involvement of the paras – and in particular the 1st REP – with the plotters.

In the 1st REP, which had been in the forefront of the fighting, events moved fast but on 24 January 1960 the leaders of the FNF forced a confrontation with the army to test its attitude by first seizing and then barricading themselves into the university and public buildings in Algiers. By mid-afternoon the Plateau des Glières was black with demonstrators when a fusillade of shots rang out and, in the ensuing massacre, fourteen *gendarmes* died and 123 people were wounded. Brought in to restore order, the paratroopers of the 10th Parachute Division, which included the 1st REP, had doubts as to which side they should take, particularly the legionnaires, who now realized that they were fighting not only for their adopted homeland but for the continued existence of the Legion itself. Many of the 1st REPs officers were prepared to cross the barricades but were held back by their commanding officer, Lieutenant-Colonel Dufour, with the words: 'You don't understand anything about revolutionary war. We've won some points. This phase is finished.'

On 29 January General de Gaulle spoke on television to such effect that his sentiments, coupled with the replacement of the largely sympathetic 10th Parachute Division by the 25th Parachute Division, resulted in the isolation of the FNF and the collapse of the revolt. At the end of 'barricades week' the *pied-noirs* ('black-foot') para-militaries were allowed to march out from behind the barricades bearing arms and accorded full honour by the 1st REP. They were conveyed in trucks to the 1st REP's barracks at Zeralda and recruited into a special unit of the Legion known as the Akazar Commando, consisting of 120 men, which did a few weeks on active service before being quietly disbanded.

With little enthusiasm, the 1st REP returned to duty in the bled (the outback), but morale slumped when the regiment was ordered not to destroy an enemy force it had trapped on the Tunisian side of the Guelma line. Lieutenant-Colonel, commanding officer of the 1st REP, now made contact with General Zeller in Paris and General Jouhard in Algiers, both of whom were plotting to further the cause of French Algeria. Dufour's outspokenness led to his posting away from the 1st REP, but he took with him the regiment's colour so that the command could not be passed on.

In the spring of 1960 de Gaulle was still urging the army to greater efforts, vowing that Algeria would never be ceded, although on 23 April Challe was promoted away from Algeria and by the summer de Gaulle was having talks with the FLN leaders, whose outcome was expressed in his radio and television broadcast on 4 November, when he declared: 'Having assumed the leadership of France, he had embarked upon a new course leading from government of Algeria by metropolitan France to an Algerian Algeria. That means an emancipated Algeria ... an Algeria which, if the Algerians wish – and I believe this to be the case – will have its own government, its own institutions and its own laws.' It was quite clear from this that he favoured Algerian independence, and such was the effect on the 1st REP that on the morning following the broadcast they did not respond to reveille, reflecting the view of their officers that there seemed little point in hunting those who would soon be Algeria's rulers. In December 1960 Lieutenant Roger Degueldre deserted, but the fact that the officers of the regiment continued to feed and house him indicated the depth of discontent not only in the 1st REP but in the minds of those opposing the idea of 'Algerian Algeria'. One of Roger Degueldre's duties was to maintain contact with the FAF (Front d'Algérie Français) which had been formed early in 1960 to replace the FNF in the aftermath of the failure at the 'barricades'.

A critical phase in the campaign developed when it became known that General de Gaulle intended to visit Algeria in December, and it was decided that during his visit FAF para-militaries would make scattered but violent attacks in Algiers which would necessitate the military being called in to help restore order. As this would involve Jouhard's three para regiments, including the 1st REP, both Algiers and de Gaulle would be seized. Unknown to the plotters – and to the potential assassins – there were several plans for his assassination, but all were thwarted by unforeseen circumstances. General de Gaulle arrived on 9 December, and on 10 December the planned FAF action took place, but the Muslim backlash the next day resulted in the FAF para-militaries being ordered to cease attacking the security forces and to assist them in protecting the *pied noirs* from the mob-mad Muslims who seemed intent on destroying the European properties and their inhabitants. The 18th Regiment of Parachutist Riflemen was called in, firing on the mob – Muslim and European – and in the confusion the projected *coup* fizzled out. The suspicions of the authorities had, however, been aroused, and as a result all the officers of the 1st REP were sent home to France, and Jouhard was discredited as a potential leader. Meanwhile de Gaulle flew home, the FLN claimed a victory, and the plotters resumed their deliberations, calling upon Lieutenant Roger Degueldre of the 1st REP to be their contact.

As the Arabs became aware of this shift of opinion, disputes arose between them and Europeans which led to sectarian killings. The French security forces could have quelled the problem but were now restrained from taking strong unilateral retaliatory action, although in keeping order both Arabs and Europeans were killed by the French.

Two very important events occurred in January 1961. Firstly the plotters created a new organization to fight for French Algeria by means of terrorism (the Secret Army Organization (OAS)) which was modelled on the French wartime resistance movement, and the FLN. The four leaders of the plot to revolt against the state – Challe, Jouhard, Salan and Zeller – now felt the time had arrived to settle the issue and in their planning believed that, once the *coup* had been successful, spearheaded by key units including the 1st REP, a chain reaction would bring overwhelming support from other units and branches of the armed forces.

The other major development was the announcement that a referendum would take place on 8 January 1961, to decide whether or not de Gaulle should be given a mandate to negotiate the future of Algeria with the FLN. In order to maintain order, the 2nd REP was transferred after Christmas 1960 to a small military camp outside Marnia, just three miles (five kilometres) from the Moroccan frontier, with the task of preventing any *fellagha* from entering Algeria and interfering with the referendum, which gave a 'yes' to de Gaulle to prepare the way for talks with the FLN. Its job done, the 2nd REP returned on 20 January 1961 to Sidi-bel-Abbès, where it remained until departing for Camp Pehau on 26 January. Located just outside the coastal town of Philippeville, Camp Pehau was not the most comfortable of permanent camps, although it had a reputation for good food and there were facilities for recreation in Philippeville itself. It was from here that the regiment would embark on operations lasting up to five days, being conveyed by truck to the nearest point to the site chosen for the advance base camp where the mess, brothel and field kitchen would be established. From there on it was marching – fast marching – from dawn until dark, with an hour's break at midday. A new recruit was not accepted until he could accomplish this physically agonizing task at least as well as his comrades.

At the time of the referendum, the 2nd REP had an establishment of about 1,000 men, of whom 800 were operationally divided into eight companies, four combat, one transport, one 'shock' and a support company (equipped with 81mm and the old British three-inch mortars) and a base company. When designated companies went out on operations, others waited in reserve ready to be transported by helicopter to the scene of the action.

Whilst on the march it was customary for the legionnaires to help themselves to any livestock they might find in the Arab *mechtas* (small farming communities), the officers turning a blind eye to such activities. At the sight of the security forces, the men usually vanished, and the destruction of property as a positive 'scorched earth' policy was fairly regularly carried out. Summary executions and the 'handling' of women were not entirely unknown occurrences on such occasions. The experiences of the Legion in Vietnam have brought about a very determined policy in regard to 'policing' the bled and continued the doctrine of 'collective responsibility' that was a major contributory factor in the increase in violence.

The bitterness and violence were not one-sided, and throughout the initial years of independence movements the French maintained their custom of raising local units of colonial troops, commanded by French officers. Algeria was no exception, and on more than one occasion units slaughtered their officers and any comrades not disposed to join them and desert to the *fellagha*. Understandably the French were keen to exact retribution and in their search for the assassins compared the identity of every killed or captured rebel with their records, the legionnaires photographing the 'remains' for this purpose.

At 19.15 hours on 20 April 1961 Challe and Zeller were smuggled aboard a French Air Force aeroplane and flown from France to Algeria, where Challe set up his command post at the para headquarters. The next day he explained the objectives in what was to become known as 'the General's *Putsch*': to seize power, finish the war against the FLN and set up a French-Algerian state on democratic lines. Later the same day Major de St-Marc, the acting regimental commander of the 1st REP, gave orders for the regiment to move, and shortly after midnight it left the barracks at Zeralda for an alleged night exercise but driving towards Algiers.

General Ferdinand Gambiez, the French commander-in-chief, suspicious of the 1st REP's intentions, drove out to the highway in an unsuccessful attempt to halt the convoy, which he followed into Algiers, witnessing legionnaires taking control of the key government buildings, including the radio station from which declarations of 'French Algeria' were made and that the army of North Africa would resist General de Gaulle's proposals for Algerian independence. Although the key buldings were taken, the plotters failed to cut all communications, and news of the *coup* was flashed to Paris and to other command centres throughout Algeria, but the hoped-for chain reaction worked against the take-over, as armed forces commanders declared themselves in favour of de Gaulle. Other Legion units which did take part were the 1st and 2nd REC, and various regular army paratroop units from the 10th Paratroop Division, under the command of General de St-Hillier, who was not involved with the plotters. On the following day, under the direction of the second-in-command, Lieutenant-Colonel Gabirot, the 2nd REP left Camp Pehau by road and arrived to a heroes' welcome in Algiers, occupying the airport after using various means of persuasion, including the liberal application of wooden batons, to remove the French marines.

With only fifty officers and 8,000 men out of a garrison estimated at 400,000, Challe had executed a brilliant *coup d'état* but the French Army, Navy and Air Force did not rally to his side, nor did the other regiments of the Legion, their attitude being summed up by General Brothier, commander of the 1st RE, who told his officers, 'The Legion is foreign by definition and will not intervene in a purely French quarrel.' Those who had promised support now sat on the fence and, with the army divided, the impetus went out of the *coup d'état*. By 26 April it was all over. Challe and Salan fled; the 1st REP returned to its barracks at Zeralda to find themselves surrounded by *gendarmes* who wisely decided that 'discretion was the better part of valour' when confronted by the enraged legionnaires. By order of the French Minister of Defence, Pierre Messmer, himself a former legionnaire, the officers became prisoners and the legionnaires were transferred to Sidi-bel-Abbès, where they were posted to other units in view of the disbandment of the 1st REP on 30 April 1961. Before leaving they blew up their barracks and tore off their medal ribbons; on the subsequent journey many deserted, numerous legionnaires – including some officers – going underground and joining the OAS. As the trucks roared out of the barracks, the legionnaires were singing Edith Piaf's '*Je ne regrette rien*' ('I regret nothing'), and the *pied noirs* wept, for they knew it was the beginning of the end.

Also disbanded were the 14th and 18th Regiments of Parachutist Riflemen, and although the 2nd REP did not suffer the same fate, it was not permitted to re-enter Camp Pehau on its return. Their transport was reduced and it was not until 5 May that they were allowed to use the camp from which they re-commenced operations. Meanwhile, General de Gaulle had commenced discussions at Evian with the Arab leaders in regard to Algerian independence.

In May Generals Salan, Jouhard and Gardy (a retired Technical Inspector of the Foreign Legion) were sentenced to death *in absentia*, although this was later commuted to a term of imprisonment. Challe and Zeller received fifteen years imprisonment, whilst Major de St-Marc of the 1st REP received ten years. All were released in 1968 as part of General de Gaulle's amnesty.

This was not by any means the end of the war, and operations continued in an atmosphere of even greater hatred, coupled with disillusionment arising from the failed *coup d'état*, so much so that disregard for human rights by French armed forces reached a new dimension after they had attacked Bizerta in Tunisia on 19 July 1961, as a reprisal for the decision of the Tunisian Government to prohibit French aircraft flying over its territory. An extract from the summary of evidence presented to the International Commission of Jurists by the Tunisian Government in September 1961 explains:

On 19 July, following the prohibition by the Tunisian Government of flights over its territory, a French attack was launched against Bizerta and its region by forces composed of parachutists and legionnaires brought in by air and sea. A battle ensued following this aggression in which the disproportionate force used by the French enabled their troops to occupy a part of the city of Bizerta. As a result, hundreds were killed and more than a thousand wounded. The fighting ceased on the evening of 22 July by the putting into effect of the provisional Resolution of the Security Council.

The utilization by the French forces of modern and highly powerful means of destruction (jet planes, napalm bombs, rockets, armoured tanks, artillery) and, especially, the violence of the parachutists and soldiers of the Foreign Legion caused a very high number of victims, particularly among the civilian population.

After considering all the evidence, on 18 September the Committee of Enquiry published its report in which the undermentioned paragraph 20 appeared:

Our general conclusion therefore is that, whatever the legal status of Bizerta may be, French armed forces between 18 and 24 July 1961, in Bizerta and within an area of about 20 kilometres of Bizerta, executed prisoners, particularly young civilian prisoners, and in some cases deliberately mutilated bodies whether before or after death, and were also guilty of other acts in violation of the provisions of the two Geneva Conventions, referred to above and in violation of any conception of Human Rights within the content of the Universal Declaration of Human Rights.

The débâcle of Bizerta was to lose for France any notions of retaining the sovereignty of the Sahara as part of the agreements being negotiated at Evian.

It was now the turn of the OAS whose real chief of action was a former Legion officer, Roger Degueldre, the leader of Commando Delta, who was determined that Algeria should remain French whatever the cost. De Gaulle's opinion of the OAS was that it consisted of 'thugs consumed by totalitarian passion ... deserters and fanatics who were the scum of the army, particularly the Foreign Legion units ...'

In Algiers and Oran a reign of terror was mounted, bringing the bomb and the gun into the daily lives of the inhabitants, with 1,500 plastic bomb attacks taking place in the spring of 1961. Many former legionnaires were involved in these attacks, including the murder of the Algiers Police Commissioner, Roger Gavoury. At a later date, Degueldre and the legionnaires who carried out this assassination were tried, convicted and executed by firing squad. On 1 November 1961 the seventh anniversary of the revolution, riots in Algiers resulted in the deaths of sixty-seven Arabs.

As negotiations towards independence proceeded at Evian, a cessation of operations for ten days commenced on 3 February 1962, a move which only increased the desertion rate of legionnaires, who often took their weapons with them as they increased the ranks of the OAS. After a period of quiet, both sides intensified the struggle in order to improve their bargaining power at the negotiating table in Evian, which ended with a cease-fire on 18 March 1962, a development not accepted by the OAS who on the 26th provoked a running battle in Algiers between the security forces and unarmed demonstrators which left forty-six dead and 200 wounded, of whom twenty died of their wounds.

On 7 April Degueldre was caught, and a similar fate befell General Salan in Algiers, on 29 April. It was nearly all over, but in a final orgy the OAS destroyed businesses, schools, public buildings, fuel stocks, shops and factories, and by the end of June out of the million French in Algeria only 100,000 remained to hear, in their adoptive country, the affirmation of the referendum which took place – without incident – in Algeria on 1 July which resulted in France's formally recognizing Algeria on 3 July 1962, the day following the declaration of independence.

Whilst I have generaly described the Algerian war in relation to the 1st and 2nd REPs, the equal part played by the other Legion regiments must not be lost sight of. The situation was aptly summed up by a former NCO of the 3rd REI: 'We weren't sat on the top of mountains scratching our arses.'

In May 1962 the 2nd REP had moved camp to Telergma and after independence found itself back in the construction business, building a new camp north of Bou-Sfer in connection with the only concessions the French secured out of the independence negotiations – a lease on the naval base at Mers-el-Kebir and oil rights in the Sahara for five years. The other units of the Legion – and the French troops in general – were given four months to 'get out', apart from those required to guard the conceded rights.

Out of boredom came a reduction in discipline and morale, accompanied by an increased rate of drinking and desertion that saw 136 legionnaires desert from the 2nd REP in the last four months of 1962. 'What of the future?' asked the legionnaires. 'What is the point in staying?' Many thought the Legion was finished.

On 24 October 1962 the 700 remaining legionnaires at

Sidi-bel-Abbès paraded to honour the Legion's dead, who would remain forever in Algeria, with the exception of General Rollet, Prince Aage of Denmark and Legionnaire Zimmerman (representing 35,000 of his comrades who had died for France) who were re-buried at Puyloubier, Provence. The silken banners captured at Tuyen Quang in 1885 were ceremonially burned as the legionnaires lit their torches and sang '*Le Boudin*'. Over the next few days the Monument to the Dead was dismantled and, together with the Legion's souvenirs, trophies and relics, was transported to Aubagne, on the outskirts of Marseilles, which had been chosen as the site for their new headquarters, where the Legion had obtained possession of the Camp de Demarde, the 1st RE leaving Algeria on 13 November 1962, to take up residence. Today the 'locals' in Sidi-bel-Abbès (where the population has dropped to less than 30,000) affect not to know of the Foreign Legion, the 1st REPs barracks at Zeralda have been bulldozed to make way for a new tourist complex. Many of the Legion's churches and cemeteries have been desecrated.

On 31 July 1962 the 2nd REC was disbanded, and its remaining effectives were absorbed by the 1st REC, which remained in Algeria based at Mers-el-Kebir until it returned to France on 17 October 1967, to its new base at the Quartier Labouche in Orange. The 2nd REI had been at Colomb Bechar from October 1962, as part of the Saharan Military Sites Command, guarding nuclear installations. At the conclusion of the tests, the regiment moved to the naval base at Mers-el-Kebir, where it remained until it returned to Aubagne on 31 January 1968, when the concession on the use of the base by the French ceased and the regiment was disbanded. At the same time as the cease-fire, the 4th REI was in the Niegrine region, and later in July it moved to Touggourt to guard oil fields. The regiment remained in the Sahara until it was disbanded on 30 April 1964, whereas the 5th REI, which was situated at Colomb Bechar, had sent its first detachments to the Pacific in the summer of 1963. In the autumn of 1962 the 13th DBLE had re-grouped in French Somaliland, where it has remained ever since.

And so the unbelievable had happened. After all the fighting and sacrifices, the political solution had resulted in France's granting independence to Algeria. After nearly 140 years, no units of the Foreign Legion remained in their adopted homeland. Soon they were to return to Africa, to Chad, in support of a Government trying to fight off rebels attempting to overthrow the legitimate regime. A major consequence of the Algerian war was the thorough modernization of the French Army, a move dictated by de Gaulle. Many famous regiments disappeared, and for a time it seemed that the end had come for the Foreign Legion, most of whose officers disappeared rapidly after 1962, posted or retired.

In December 1962, however, it was announced that the Legion would undergo major changes designed to make it an important part of the French Army, with certain units having elite status with specialized sections in techniques of survival and of subversive and guerrilla warfare. 'We're back in business' was the word, and it counted – morale improved almost overnight: everyone wanted to get on with the future.

Reminders of the Legion's long association with the Magrheb still occur in the most unusual places. A professor of the Sahara recalls how, on a sunny morning in January 1983, he was battling his way down the inhospitable and extremely rough *piste* linking central Algerian Amguid – a ghost town now boasting a garrisoned fort and a few huts – towards Zaouatallaz, the old Fort Gardel, *en route* towards Djanet in the Tassili-N-Ajjer. At a point shown by the occasional metal route-markers, some 200 miles (320 kilometres) from Amguid, his companions wanted to check for traces of an ancient track joining from the north-east, issuing out of the Massif d'Adrar. Whilst the Professor was turning back towards the cars, something attracted his attention. Almost buried in the coarse sand lay what looked like a crumpled piece of metal wire, its identity quite inexplicable until he picked it up. Before their astonished gaze materialized the rear part of a metal button; turning it over, they made out two words carefully picked out in relief around the outer edge, 'Légion Etrangère'.

What had been the fate of the man who wore the uniform from which the button had been lost? Had he undertaken the same sort of search as they, whiling away a few minutes, hours or even days, possibly waiting beside a wrecked vehicle? Or, like Laperrine, for help which came too late? Or was he just another victim of a routine military fiasco, marched up before his company commander and sentenced to some trivial penalty for losing this item of his equipment?

8 Chad and the Horn of Africa

Following the departure of the Legion from Algeria, a number of organizational changes took place. The 1st RE (which had dropped the 'I' suffix in July 1955) became the reception and training unit on behalf of the central controlling organization, the Autonomous Group of the Foreign Legion (GALE), which had itself been formed in 1950. It established itself at Aubagne in its existing role, but the Technical Inspectorate (ITLE), which had been based in Paris since its establishment in July 1957, was disbanded on 31 July 1964, and its functions were transferred to Aubagne, where the senior command function of the Legion has remained. However, in September 1972 the Autonomous Group of the Foreign Legion became 'the Group of the Foreign Legion' and, at the time of writing, the Legion is part of the 5th Military Region.

The 2nd REP moved to a new base on Corsica at Calvi, whilst the 2nd REI, which had been reformed on 1 September 1972, was also based on Corsica, having established itself at bases in Corte and Boni-Facio, where it had two functions – instruction and 'quick intervention'. The former was designated 'the Instruction Group of the Foreign Legion' (GILE), undertaking all basic and most specialist training. Problems caused by deserting recruits led to the instruction unit transferring first to Puyloubier and Orange in October 1976 and to Castelnaudary with effect from 1 September 1977, with the designation 'Instruction Regiment of the Foreign Legion' (RILE). On 1 June 1980 the RILE inherited the flag and traditions of the old 4th REI and became the 4th RE, based at the Quartier Lapasset at Castelnaudary, where it carries out basic training for recruits and continuation training for NCOs. In addition to the firing range, assault course and sports ground, each company has its own farm, and the Legion has recently built a new camp with firing ranges and sports ground. Known as the Quartier Capitaine Danjou, it is just outside Castelnaudary at 'Les Cheminières'. The advanced and specialist training of all ranks – including officers – is undertaken by GILE and has continued as a function of the 2nd REI, as has its 'quick intervention' role for overseas action – Operational Group of the Foreign Legion (GOLE), which consists of a headquarters and three rifle companies. In November 1983 the regiment left Corsica, and it is now based at the Quartier Vallongue near Nîmes, to the west of Marseilles.

From Algeria, the 3rd REI went to Diego-Suarez in Madagascar in 1962, where it specialized in amphibious operations and developed training for troops involved in tropical conditions. In November 1967 the regiment detached a company to the Comoro Islands which set up bases on the rock of Dzaoudzi on the small island of Pamandze, off Mayotte, and at Moroni, the islands' capital on Great Comoro. Known as 'the Foreign Legion Detachment of the Comoros (DLEC), it remained on the islands when the 3rd REI left Madagascar on 25 August 1973, to take up positions in French Guyana. On 1 April 1976 the Comoros became independent, but Mayotte chose to become an overseas department of France, which resulted in the detached company changing its name to 'the Foreign Legion Detachment of Mayotte' (DLEM). The legionnaires remained at Dzaoudzi, although construction of a new barracks is being undertaken at Kwali. Mayotte has a population of 50,000 and occupies a strategic position at the opening of the Mozambique channel into the Indian Ocean, so it is not surprising that units of the French Marine and Air Force are also based on the island. However, all armed forces come under the control of the officer commanding the DLEM, who also has the responsibility for maintaining the sovereignty of France and its way of life in this area of command.

Arriving in French Guyana at the capital of Cayenne, the 3rd REI based three companies at the European Space Centre at Kourou, where the Legion constructed the Ariane rocket site for which they now provide security. The headquarters company and two combat companies are based at the Quartier Forget, a collection of modern buildings on the outskirts of the town. They are responsible for the port installations at Kourou where the three LCMs are based. The equipment company is based at Camp Szuts, Regina. Legionnaires are also involved in the construction of 125 miles (201 kilometres) of the Route de l'Est, which is part of the Trans-American highway system and when completed will link

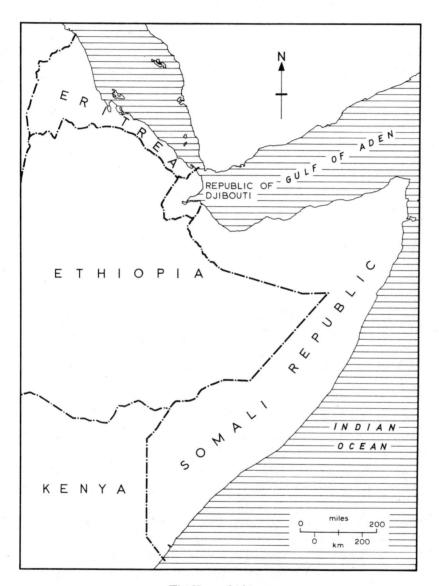

The Horn of Africa

Cayenne with St-Georges. Here the Legion maintains a
detachment at Camp Caporal Bernet, consisting of a lieutenant,
NCOs and thirty legionnaires. Rotated every two months, the
detachment mounts regular patrols on the Oyapock river which
threads its way through the jungle close to the border with Brazil.
All legionnaires are posted to St-Georges to undertake practical
training in the jungle, which includes the art of survival, following a
basic course at the Jungle Training School close to Kourou. These
exercises from St-Georges can last up to forty-five days at a time,
and in 1985 the Legion's latest formation, the 6th Foreign
Engineering Assault Regiment (6th REG) visited Guyana, landing
at Kourou. After a period of acclimatization, the legionnaires
undertook the jungle-familiarization course, after which they took
part in a combat exercise with the 3rd REI before returning to
France.

Whilst the majority of legionnaires withdrew to their new bases in
metropolitan France leaving only the agreed regiments in the
enclave of Mers-el-Kebir and those required to guard the Saharan
oil fields and the nuclear test sites, the 13th DBLE was taking up
positions in French Somaliland, where it has remained ever since.
This small country of scrubland and desert which measures some
8,400 square miles (21,760 square kilometres) had been a French
'protectorate' since 1888 and is almost entirely bordered by
Ethiopia, with a small area on the south-east border which gives
access to the Somali Democratic Republic, which achieved
independence on 26 June 1960, uniting British Somaliland and the
former Somalia. The French were determined to resist the new
republic's stated intention of incorporating French Somaliland,
whose population had voted in 1958 to remain an overseas territory
of France. For many years the interests of France and Ethiopia were
closely linked in regard to commerce, which was served by the
railway which linked Addis Ababa to the port of Djibouti. The
incessant wars over the past ten years have, however, led to the
railway being badly damaged and consequently of little use.
    However, the move towards independence gathered momentum
and a number of violent clashes occurred between Afar and Ise
tribesmen. The situation worsened considerably when a group of
FLCS terrorists (Front de la Côte des Somalis) hijacked a school
bus at Loyoda conveying children of French military personnel.

The incident occurred on the morning of 3 February 1976, just as the two school buses were returning the children from primary and secondary schools. Suddenly four armed men boarded the bus conveying about thirty primary school children and ordered the driver off at gun point, a terrorist taking over. At the approach to the police control post 300 yards (270 metres) from the Djibouti City exit, the terrorist who was driving the bus accelerated and smashed through the barrier, causing a *gendarme* to leap out of the way, and drove off at high speed towards Somalia.

The *gendarme* alerted the authorities and police at the next post, some twenty-five miles (forty kilometres) from Djibouti (near the frontier with Somalia), who placed a vehicle across the road to obstruct the passage of the bus. On arrival, the terrorist halted the bus with the door open in which he held a young boy with a pistol at his head. Shouting to the *gendarmes*, the terrorist threatened: 'Attention! If you approach, I fire. This child will be the first to die of all those here.' He then sent the child with a message to the chief of the post, containing the terrorists' demands:

i) Release all their comrades from detention.
ii) Restoration of their seized armaments.
iii) Immediate independence without conditions.
iv) Immediate departure of all French security forces.
v) Refuse – and the children would be executed.

French public opinion supported the Government's view that it should not concede to the terrorists' demands, but nor could they allow the terrorists to execute the children. Meanwhile, the Intervention Group of the Gendarmerie Nationale (GIGN) under the command of Lieutenant Prouteau flew to Djibouti where the chief of the commando offered to substitute himself as a hostage in place of the children, but this was refused by the terrorists. However, towards evening they agreed that Jehanne Bru, an energetic and courageous woman who was a civilian staff member at the Djibouti base, might join the children to look after them. Finding them excited and nervous, she was able to comfort them and distribute food and drink.

Meanwhile, General Brasart had alerted his troops, including a company of the 2nd REP under the command of Captain Soubirou, who set up positions near the bus. But the terrorists demanded the road be cleared and the bus was driven nearer the Somalia frontier. Again the chief of the commando offered to take the children's place but this was refused by the terrorists who restated their intentions of executing the children unless a favourable response was received from the French Government.

At 13.00 hours General Brasert decided to deploy AMLs of the 13th DBLE but at 16.00 hours the school bus was observed being driven to a point in front of the Somalia army post, making it difficult to fire on the bus without involving the Somalia military. The legionnaires keeping the bus under observation were certain that the terrorists were receiving reinforcements, and it was confirmed by Lieutenant Proteau of the newly arrived GIGN that one terrorist was behind the bus, three were inside, two patrolling in its vicinity and a sixth was on the balcony on the frontier post.

Just after Jehanne Bru had distributed her sandwiches, the security forces attacked, the three sections of the 2nd REP rushing towards their objectives, which resulted in two of the terrorists being shot dead in the opening shots. A group of the enemy who tried to attack an AML wounded Lieutenant Doucet but Staff Sergeant Raoul eliminated them. Then the snipers of the 2nd Section of the 13th DBLE fired on the bus, covering Corporal Larking, who was first on the bus. Corporal Lemoine shot a Somalian without touching the child near him and Staff Sergeant Jorand shot the third terrorist.

Twenty-one children were immediately evacuated through the bus windows onto police vehicles and the wounded were evacuated by helicopter to Djibouti – five children, the conductor and Jehanne Bru were slightly hurt. A little girl who had sat on the conductor's knee was killed and another died of her wounds; she was buried at Aubagne near her grandfather, a former Legion NCO. Although shots were exchanged by the legionnaires with Somali troops, who opened fire from across the border, the action was over in half an hour and delivered the hostages from their captors without escalating the incident with the Somali Government, but regrettably at the cost of the death of two children. The last comment should be that of one of the children, Marie Line, who, when asked why she had looked out of the window to watch the legionnaires attack, replied, 'It was such fun, mademoiselle, it was such fun!'

The resulting political upheaval hastened the move for independence, which was achieved at midnight on 26 June 1977, when the Republic of Djibouti was proclaimed. The new nation has a heavy dependence on France for aid and defence, which is undertaken by the Legion, supported by units of the French Navy and Air Force. All these units have their principal bases at Djibouti; that occupied by the Legion – the Quartier Gabode – is close to the airport. (In addition to the 13th DBLE, to which one squadron of the 1st REC is permanently attached, other units, including the 2nd REP, undertake tours of duty in the republic.)

Constant border problems are experienced, particularly as a result of the widespread famine in Africa and from Ethiopia's conflicts with Somalia and Eritrea, which have bought an inflow of refugees, who have swollen the country's population from 100,000 to 250,000 in under ten years. Most of these immigrants have settled in shanty towns outside the port and capital city of Djibouti.

Recreation for legionnaires in Djibouti is provided at Moucha, one of a small group of islands just off the coast in the Gulf of Aden. Transport to and from the island is undertaken in one of the Legion's 60 hp Zodiac rubber launches. Whilst at Moucha, the legionnaires look after themselves, cooking, relaxing and fishing and, whilst there is no formal discipline, the respect attached to rank is maintained by the fact that each individual is addressed by his title.

The short leases retained in Algeria by the French necessitated their establishing alternative facilities for nuclear testing, and French Polynesia was chosen. Following a decision by the French Ministry of Defence in August 1963, the 5th Mixed Pacific Regiment (5th RMP) was formed on 1 October 1963, consisting of legionnaires and French Army engineers. On 30 November 1963 the 5th REI – which had sent a detachment to Tahiti in June 1963 and another to Mururoa in September of that year – was disbanded, and on 9 December 1963 the 5th RMP inherited its traditions together with the regiment's colours. By 1964 the regiment was constructing sites in Tahiti, Mururoa, Hao and Rapa and progress was such that on 24 August 1968 the 'first' French nuclear bomb was successfully tested.

It seems probable that the French decision to have an independent nuclear capability was influenced by the failure of the USA to support Britain and France at the time of the Suez operation in 1956. When France pulled out of NATO in 1966, de Gaulle stated: 'In 1956, at the time of the Suez affair, neither France nor

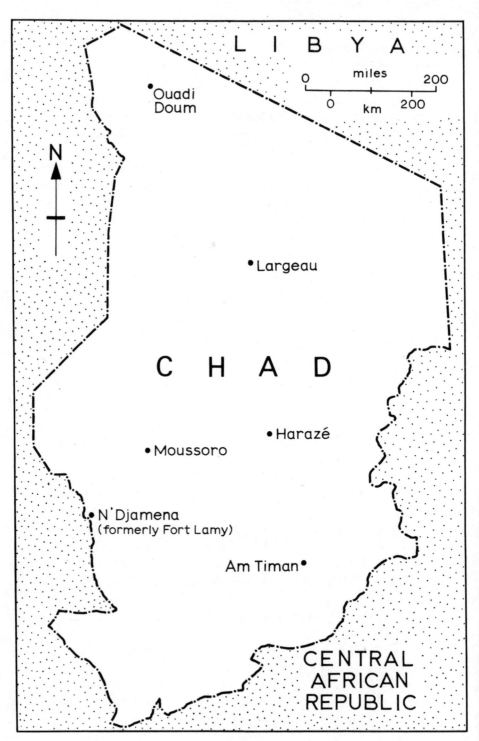

Chad

Britain had been attacked by Egypt. When Marshal Bulganin, in the name of the Soviet Union, threatened to send rockets on Paris and London, the United States showed by their attitude that their obligations to NATO did not enter into the matter.'

At the Pacific test centre, the Legion has maintained its traditions of construction, and in addition it assumed the responsibility for the maintenance of vehicles and machinery, including the operation of power stations, and the production of fresh water and security.

Following the successful test, a reorganization of the Legion's functions took place in 1969, and for the next six years extensive construction work was undertaken on the atolls scattered across the Pacific. By 1976 the 5th RMP was based at Mururoa, where the electro-mechanical company became a water-power company, with a support company based at Hao, which was disbanded in 1977 when all the resources were brought together in Mururoa. Since that date, a small transport unit and a section of the water-power company have remained on Tahiti with only very small detachments remaining on the outlying atolls. On 10 July 1985 – the same month as the 5th RMP became the 5th RE – the Greenpeace environmental pressure-group boat, the *Rainbow Warrior*, was sunk in Auckland harbour, New Zealand, whilst allegedly preparing to sail into the area of the French nuclear test site. President Mitterand of France announced that any such attempts would be resisted by force.

Another small French colony which had achieved self-government (unfortunately in a climate of disorder and anarchy) was Chad, and as part of the arrangements, a defence agreement had been concluded with France. Chad is an ethnicly divided country, with the legal government in the hands of the Negro-Muslim people. Early in 1969 this government found itself threatened by two rebel movements, one operating on the eastern frontier from suspected bases in Sudan, the other with its main support from the Tubu tribal party in the central Saharan area. In both cases the hand of 'outside forces' was discernible in the inspiration and support of the rebels.

In April 1969 General de Gaulle responded to an appeal for help from President Tombalbaye by sending in a tactical headquarters and two rifle companies of the 2nd REP under the command of

Major de Chastenet, to restore order in the country. They flew from Calvi (Corsica) to Fort Lamy in Chad and transformed themselves into motorized companies with the aid of local vehicles they acquired for the purpose. One section became horse cavalry for patrolling in country unsuited to wheeled vehicles. The parachutists were supported by three Tripacer observation aircraft, an Alouette helicopter for the commanding officer, one Pirate helicopter 'gunship' and six H34 transports, which gave the legionnaires a high degree of mobility.

Three important actions occurred in the first six months of intervention. The first was on the road to Mangalmé where rebels ambushed a convoy of vehicles, and in September 1969 the 2nd Company was airlifted from Fort Lamy to Faya-Largeau to repulse a large band of rebels who had attacked the Chadian Army. Captain Aubert and his legionnaires pursued the rebels, but it was several days before they found a group of eight in the oasis at Bedo, together with the rebel chief for the province of Borkou, Ennedi and Tibesti. Guided by one of the Tripacers, he continued the pursuit to a village where another four rebels were captured.

The third action occurred during the following month, when Major de Chastenet, whilst returning from a visit to the prefect of Am Tinan, observed from his aircraft a rebel group with horses. After instructing the pilot to continue the flight as though the rebels had not been sighted, he called by radio on his units to mount an operation. Helicopters transported a section of legionnaires to the scene but the rebels took up positions in a small wood, where they were observed and fired upon by the crew of the Pirate helicopter gunship. This highly successful operation resulted in sixty-eight rebels being put out of the combat.

On 25 October 1969 Colonel Lacaze landed at Fort Lamy with the regiment's colour, his staff and reinforcements from the 2nd REP, together with a motorized company formed by the 1st RE. These reinforcements led to a considerable escalation in the level of operations, and Operation Cantharide in November resulted in the capture of several weapons. This was followed in December by Operation Coccinelle, undertaken by the CMLE, which accounted for thirty or so rebels. Finally, on Christmas Day the 3rd Company of the 2nd REP uncovered about twenty weapons following a search of Harazé.

In April 1970 Colonel Lacaze and EMT 1 returned to Calvi and were replaced in Chad by EMT 2 under the command of Major Malaterre. Deciding to march rather than ride, the companies led a nomadic life as they patrolled on foot. During October the Reconnaissance and Support Company (CEA) of Captain Wabinski on operations in the east of Chad were airlifted to Zouar in the north-west, where the Chadian Army garrison was encircled by rebels who were also occupying the Leclerc pass through to Libya. The Chadian troops could not assure the security of the airstrip some 3 miles (five kilometres) to the south, and its capture would require a bold and dangerous assault.

Disregarding the risks, the French aircrew touched down, not stopping whilst the legionnaires disembarked. The rebels, surprised by this audacious move, offered little resistance, with the result that by evening the legionnaires had made contact with their column, which had arrived by road. Using the hours of darkness for cover, the Wabinski Company, guided by a section of the Chadian Army, infiltrated the Leclerc pass, causing the rebels to retreat into the caves, with the result that the battle, which continued throughout the following day, ended in a stalemate. However, Captain Wabinski again profited from the hours of darkness which enabled a company of Chadian parachutists to be flown in, in helicopters, and they, with the legionnaires, drove the rebels out of the caves, killing forty-one and capturing two machine-guns, two automatic rifles and nineteen rifles. Pressing home the attack, the Wabinski Company reopened the Leclerc pass, the section of Warrant Officer Fayolle being air-lifted by helicopter to the rebel base at Goubone, where they captured one machine-gun, two AA52 machine-guns, six rifles and a stock of miscellaneous armaments together with a quantity of documents. The Legion casualties numbered one dead and six wounded.

In the following month two sections of the 2nd REP and two sections of the CMLE fought the final battle of this intervention when they attacked the Troubbous rebels retreating into the caves in the area of Fada, an area unsuitable for air attack. The legionnaires attacked the caves one by one, guided by their comrades on the opposite side of the gorge. Fifty rebels were put *hors de combat* as a result of this action, and a Bren gun, a Piat and several rifles were captured; but one legionnaire was killed and twelve were wounded.

These skirmishes gradually wore down the rebel bands, but

whereas by early 1970 the central and southern areas of Chad were reasonably quiet, the clashes in the north were much more violent. However, the Legion accomplished its task to the declared satisfaction of Chad's leader, President Tombalbaye, and in April 1970 the bulk of the 2nd REP returned to Corsica, followed by the reconnaissance and heavy weapons company, together with the CMLE, who returned in December.

The second intervention commenced on 3 March 1978, with the departure of the Tacaud detachment which consisted of twenty-five officers, NCOs and legionnaires of the 2nd REP to act as a cadre for the Chadian Army, who were now opposing rebels led by Goukouni supported and equipped by Colonel Gadaffi of Libya. Shortly after their arrival at N'djamena (formerly Fort Lamy), the Tacaud detachments were despatched to Mongo to assist the garrison defending the town. In May the commanding officer, Lieutenant-Colonel Lhopitallier, mounted a reconnaisance into the desert during which he and his troops travelled 95 miles (150 kilometres) in three hours to the town of Ati, which had been occupied overnight by Goukouni's troops.

As the leading elements approached l'Oued Batha, they were attacked by 81mm and 120mm mortars, 106mm cannons and automatic weapons. Taking cover, the legionnaires and Chadian troops waited whilst Lhopitallier called for reinforcements by helicopter from Mongo and by Jaguar ground-attack aircraft based at N'djamena. Guided onto their objectives by the legionnaires, the aircraft destroyed the mortar battery and numerous anti-tank guns, permitting the attackers to deploy inside l'Oued Batha. Later in the month a squadron of the 1st REC arrived in Chad and travelled the 125 miles (200 kilometres) to Moussuro, arriving during the night to join the troops of Lhopitallier who were to the south of Bathau.

At 05.00 hours on 20 May the squadron's Commanding Officer, Captain Ivanoff, deployed his Panhard AMLs, which effectively used their 90mm cannons against the emplacements of the rebels. When the day ended, the legionnaires counted one hundred bodies and captured considerable quantities of armaments, including 106mm and 75mm recoilless cannons, and 120mm and 81mm mortars – all supplied by Libya. A week later the Tacaud and Ivanoff detachments were again in action in a violent combat which lasted two days, at Djadda some 32 miles (50 kilometres) north of

Ati. Amongst the weapons captured here were three Russian-made RPG7 rocket-launchers.

Four months after its arrival, the Tacaud detachment returned to Calvi, but the 1st REC strengthened its presence in Chad, with its squadrons mounting offensive patrols, mainly in the north, the remainder of the country having returned to normal. The 2nd Squadron of the 1st REC made a chance interception of a small group of rebels, capturing a few modern weapons, before they were replaced by the 2nd REI. On 24 November 1978 the 7th Company, after several days of pursuit, caught up with a band of rebels, and in a vicious, close-quarter battle twenty rebels were killed and three wounded. In September 1979 this intervention ceased, and the legionnaires returned via Cameroon, their skills having received considerable recognition.

In August 1983 the Legion was once again called upon to intervene in Chad, with other French forces, as part of Operation Manta. This followed a request from President Hissène Habré, whose government was once again threatened by his rival, Goukouni Oueddi, again supported by Colonel Gadaffi. Initially the actions took place in the north of the country, but the affair took on a new importance because the rebels were supported on several occasions by the Libyan Air Force.

The initial French presence had been marines of the 8th RPIMa (Marine Regiment of Infantry Parachutists) who were relieved in January 1984 by the 2nd REP, based at Biltine, some 95 miles (150 kilometres) from the frontier with Sudan. A squadron of AMX-10RCs of the 1st REC was based at Ati to support French forces in the event of an enemy attack, but as no significant actions occurred, the legionnaires left Chad in May 1984. However, the deployment of the intervention force in the difficult climatic conditions was a good test both for the troops involved in the utilization of modern equipment and the action of the Rapid Action Force (FAR).

In the two decades since leaving Algeria, the Legion has spent the greater part of its time in construction rather than combat, but its high standard of training has brought international recognition of its professionalism, particularly from the successful outcome of its involvement in international incidents referred to in the next chapter. The important point to remember, however, is that, whilst the backbone of the Legion is its 'foreign' legionnaires, the officers in the main are French, and the Legion is there to act in accordance with the policy and direction of the French Government.

9 *En Avant la Légion!*

Between 1971 and 1978 a legionnaire could fulfil his contract without firing a shot in anger. This is precisely what occurred in the 'generation' between the legionnaires returning from Chad in 1971 and those in action in Kolwezi when the 2nd REP rescued a large number of civilians from murderous Katangan rebels.

Kolwezi is a mining town in the Shaba province of northern Zaire, a country which had seen considerable bloodshed at the time of independence, but the Katangan secession crisis was just a memory, and the security of the civilian population, both black and white, was supposedly assured by the presence of the Zairean regular army. However, at dawn on 13 May 1978 between 1,500 and 4,000 Katangan 'Tiger' rebels of the Congolese National Liberation Front (FNLC) crossed the border from nearby Angola with the intention of re-possessing Shaba province, during the course of which they captured Kolwezi. At the rebels' approach, the Zairean soldiers fled, leaving the civilians – particularly the 3,000 Europeans – at the mercy of the rebels who, not content with a military campaign, went on an orgy of destruction and looting, during the course of which they murdered, raped and tortured.

By one of the few instances of good fortune on that unhappy day, the radio operator employed by the Gécamines Mining Company was able to pass a message to the company's office at Kinshasa, from which the directors informed the French Ambassador, Colonel Larzul (the military attaché) and Colonel Gras (head of a technical assistance scheme). The officers called for assistance from western Governments, particularly Belgium, which had been the colonial power until independence. Fearful of the consequences, the Belgians procrastinated and declined to play more than a strictly humanitarian role. The French Government, however, working in conjunction with its representatives in Kinshasa, responded to an appeal by President Mobuto of Zaire to the French President, Giscard d'Estaing, who became convinced by 17 May that there was a real possibility of a massacre. He therefore ordered that the 2nd REP in Calvi, Corsica, be placed on standby and all detached units and individuals be immediately recalled, enabling the commanding officer, Colonel Erulin, to report later the same afternoon that his regiment was ready for 'Operation Leopard'. At 01.30 hours on 18 May, he received his movement orders, and at 08.00 the bulk of the 2nd REP was at Corsica's Solenzara airport.

As mentioned in Chapter 8, the Legion is on call for such emergencies, each of which has unique problems to be overcome, in the operations implementation. On this occasion it was distance in relation to time when a security leak might have brought about the massacre of Europeans feared by the French. But such was the speed with which the 2nd REP acted that by 23.30 hours on 18 May Colonel Erulin had arrived in Kinshasa, to be followed a few hours later by the 650 parachutists of the headquarters, four rifle companies and the reconnaissance platoon. Transferring from their DC-8s to four C-130s and one C-160 transport aircraft, their locally issued American parachutes gave some difficulty on account of their non-compatibility with the parachutists' equipment and the need for eighty men to be crammed into a C-130 which normally carried sixty-six. The headquarters and three rifle companies formed the first lift in the aircraft, which took off from Kinshasa at 11.00 hours on 19 May, arriving over Kolwezi (a distance of 800 miles – about 1,300 kilometres) at 15.00 hours. The drop zone was to the north-east of the old town, and the parachutists jumped from a height of 600 feet (183 metres) onto unreconnoitred terrain defended by an unknown number of enemy troops who, in the event, were quickly overcome by the legionnaires. It was almost exactly twenty-four years since the unit's last battalion drop over Dien Bien Phu.

Following a confused firefight, the legionnaires pressed on with their advance against dispersed groups of FLNC until they reached their first objective, the old town, which they quickly cleared of defenders before setting free from amongst the wrecked buildings a number of hostages, who joined up with the few who had managed to hide from the Katangan rebels. By nightfall most of the objectives had been taken and, despite several nights without sleep, the legionnaires beat off scattered attacks by maurauding groups of the FNLC, some of whom were still patrolling the area of the new town. At dawn on 20 May the 4th Company, equipped with mortars, together with the recce platoon, dropped to join their comrades, with whom they cleared the new town, proceeding to the native quarter of Marika, where they had to fight house to house in several bitter skirmishes which had an extra sense of urgency because the rebels were beginning to execute their remaining hostages. A fierce firefight then ensued in the northern Metal-Shaba suburbs. Until that point the Legion's casualties had been mercifully light, with only one killed, but this engagement resulted in the death of four more legionnaires. After a heavy mortar barrage, the rebels were forced to withdraw, leaving behind quantities of weapons, including mortars, machine-guns and recoilless rifles and eighty dead.

Belgian troops and medical teams arrived on 20 May, the day on which Colonel Erulin was able to organize the first hostage evacuation. The second echelon of the 2nd REP arrived with the regiments' vehicles, flying direct to Shaba provincial capital, Lubumbashi, in US Air Force C5 and C141 transports. Their vehicles were then driven the 200 miles (320 kilometres) to Kolwezi (enabling the Legion to return those they had borrowed from Gécamines), and on 28 May, after patrols and sharp clashes at Kapata and Luilu, the 2nd REP moved back to Lubumbashi. Between 21 and 28 May the Legion had the use of the Gécamines aircraft in addition to their own, enabling the 2nd REP to extend the range of patrols, which caused the rebels to abandon their campaign and withdraw into Angola. This enabled the legionnaires to leave Zaire, and by 4 June they were back in Corsica for a cost of five dead and twenty-five wounded, although they had killed 250 FNLC and captured 163. The legionnaires had saved the lives of 2,000 hostages, which earned the 2nd REP worldwide admiration. The final act in the drama was the arrival on 8 June in Shaba of the African Multi-National Force who were required to stabilize the situation following the departure of the legionnaires.

The next four years were spent in training and construction, but in 1982 the Legion became involved in a matter of great international importance. Whilst the origins of the strife in Lebanon are not a subject for this book, the French involvement in 1982 had its origins in air attacks made in 1974 and 1980 by Israel, and reprisals from Palestinian positions in south Lebanon. Since 1976 the Syrian army had based troops in Lebanon, and by 1982 it was estimated that between 15,000 and 20,000 Palestinian forces, well equipped with artillery, armoured fighting vehicles and modern small arms, were on Lebanese territory. These circumstances gave rise to the Israeli Government's decision to finish the matter once and for all, and on 6 June 1982 the Israeli Defence Forces launched 'Operation Peace for Galilee' by invading Lebanon along a sixty-three-mile (100-kilometre) stretch of the frontier.

On 24 June 1982 the French Government presented a resolution to the Security Council of the United Nations that all foreign troops should be evacuated from Lebanon and that the Lebanese forces should be reinforced by troops from the International Peace-Keeping Force. Arising from subsequent negotiations on 29 July 1982, Yassar Arafat, the leader of the Palestine Liberation Organization (PLO) agreed in principle to withdraw his forces from Lebanon. However, the Israeli artillery and Air Force continued to attack West Beirut, and by 12 August the Israeli armies encircled the city. On the night of 3 August Yassar Arafat accepted the evacuation of his troops provided that it was supervised by French troops and that the PLO forces could take their personal weapons with them. As a result, on the night of 18/19 August a detachment of the 2nd REP left their base at Calvi for the airport at Bastia, entrusted with three tasks: 1. Assuring the physical security of the Palestine personnel during their departure from Beirut under the direction of the Lebanese army; 2. Assuring the physical security of the other inhabitants of Beirut; 3. Supporting the restoration of the sovereignty and authority of the Lebanese Government in all regions.

And so began, on 19 August, Operation Epaulard 1, commencing as the 1st and 3rd Companies of the 2nd REP boarded a DC-8 of COTAM (Military Air Transport Command) at Bastia airport in Corsica. From there they flew to the British base at Larnaca in Cyprus, transferring to the French transport ship *Dives* for the escorted crossing to Lebanon. At 06.30 hours on 21 August the first legionnaire on the quay at Beirut was Lieutenant Charles Guermeur, aged twenty-eight, at the head of his section. The quays were thronged with troops and journalists. The first hitch was the presence of Israeli troops, who had prevented Lebanese troops moving into the port area, stating that they, the Israelis, would assume the protection of the legionnaires. A vehement protest from the French Ambassador led to the Israeli troops moving away, enabling the legionnaires to take up their positions to separate the Lebanese army, the Israelis and the PLO with such expedition that by 07.30 they were in total control of the port. Meanwhile, in two return flights their fifty-seven vehicles were flown in from Bastia and Solenzara by C-160s and a jumbo jet of Air France, thereby enabling the 1st Company to contact the PLO after an unexpected meeting with the Syrians.

Soon afterwards the arrival of the first PLO members in the port area was announced by intense gunfire from small arms fired into the air, accompanied by the shouting of political slogans in an atmosphere of a victory celebration as they embarked on their Greek evacuation ship. The second phase of the movement of French troops commenced on 21 August as the 1st Squadron of the RICM (Marine Regiment of Infantry and Tanks) with elements of the 9th RCS of the 9th DIMa (9th Armoured Regiment of the 9th Marine Infantry Division) with armoured fighting vehicles landing at Beirut the next day, being joined on 25 August by 194 men of the 3rd RPIMa and a section consisting of 300 men of the 17th RGP (Regiment of Engineer Parachutists).

By 25 August the 2nd REP had taken up positions outside the port where they were able to inspect the strong fortifications which had enabled the PLO to withstand the Israeli assault, the 3rd Company taking up positions for the surveillance of the camps occupied by the families of the PLO fighters who had left Beirut.

On the final day of the evacuation, 30 August, Yassar Arafat was the last to arrive, having demanded and obtained a personal escort consisting of senior officers of all the armies involved in the Lebanon peace-keeping forces, including Colonel Janvier, commanding officer of the 2nd REP. This group then travelled in the vehicle preceding that occupied by Yassar Arafat, who, just prior to the final checkpoint, alighted from his vehicle to review his supporters and salute the flag of the PLO. During the ensuing walkabout, Yassar Arafat was so engulfed by his enthusiastic supporters that Colonel Janvier of the 2nd REP stood on top of his jeep to keep the PLO leader in view as he boarded the *Atlantis* to almost hysterical cheering. Several minutes later, complete with an escort of French and American naval vessels, the Greek ship left Beirut, and so the Palestinians peacefully departed from Lebanon. In twelve days the 2nd REP had facilitated the evacuation of 9,000 PLO, 2,500 soldiers of the ALP and 2,000 soldiers of the Syrian Army.

Following the evacuation, the CCS (the Headquarters and Services Company) of the 2nd REP was relieved at the port by the American 32nd Marine Amphibious Unit after which the legionnaires encamped at the Residence des Pins and the 'hippodrome voisin'. The legionnaires also resumed their role as builders, reconstructing the defensive wall which enclosed the residence of the French Ambassador.

Although the mandate of the multi-national peacekeeping force had another month to elapse, the election of Bechir Gemayel as President of the Lebanese Government decided the French to withdraw their forces, and on 13 September 1982 the legionnaires were transferred by eight Super Frelon helicopters to the aircraft-carrier *Foch*, their vehicles being loaded at the port on the *Dives* and the *L'Orage*.

The next day President Gemayel was assassinated, and on the following day the Israelis occupied West Beirut, which was followed on 17 and 18 September by the massacre of civilian Palestinians in the camps at Sabra and Chatila. From his base in Tunisia, Yassar Arafat again appealed to the French Government, requesting them to intervene and send forces to protect Palestinian families in Beirut. In accepting the invitation, the French Government did so as part of a multi-national security force which contained detachments from the USA, Britain and Italy. In May 1983 the French 31st Brigade, under the command of General Coullon, landed in Lebanon with elements of the 1st REC and the 2nd REI who deployed their companies in various positions in West Beirut. The 5th Company was located near the beach and the famous hotels which had been ravaged by the war. This company was also responsible for the security of the French Embassy. On the other extreme, the 6th Company took up positions near the Palestinian refugee camps at Sabra and Chatila, where they experienced at first hand the horrible conditions under which the inhabitants were living during the ordeal of the Israeli bombardment.

The 7th Company took on the role of instructors for the Lebanese Army, establishing a Commando Training Centre in the mountains, where they trained the Lebanese 2nd Battalion in the art of helicopter operations as a result of an arrangement between the French and Lebanese Governments that the presence of the French troops in Lebanon should not be entirely to the benefit of the Palestinians. The CEA took up positions in the south of Beirut in the area of Sabra from where they could keep the airport under surveillance.

Five legionnaires of the 2nd REI died during the course of the Lebanese intervention, Corporals Amaioro and Rides and legionnaires Stitjovic, Le Jeune and Peigney.

The participation of two squadrons of the 1st REC came fifty-eight years after its last visit to the Levant. Travelling by Boeing 747, the legionnaires landed at Beirut airport on 1 July 1983, where they relieved the armoured regiment of the 9th Marine Infantry Division. The legionnaires brought with them their new AMX 10-RCs, presenting a contrast to their previous sojourn in the area when their equipment had been 1920s Panhard AMLs. One of the problems faced by the legionnaires in patrolling the streets of Beirut with their AMX 10-RCs was the use by the many and varied combatants of very similar equipment – particularly vehicles – which often resulted in exchanges of fire, particularly at night. Legionnaires of the 1st and 4th RE constituted the section of protection which was accommodated in the old residence of the French Ambassador. At the end of September 1983 the 31st Brigade was relieved by the 11th Parachute Division, elements of the 2nd REI landing at Istres on 16 September, followed by the 1st REC, the last contingent returning on 30 September 1983.

Today the Foreign Legion's command centre is established at the headquarters in Aubagne, the base of the 1st RE which is responsible for the function of the Legion's services and recruitment. The 1st RE comes under the direct orders of the Legion's commanding general and in its administrative role has departments dealing with personnel, statistics, recruiting, welfare and the Legion's band.

The 1st RE has a headquarters company, a Command and Services Company (CCS), a Company of Training and Cadres (CIC) and three companies of recruits (CEV). There is a Foreign Legion Company of Transit (CTLE) based at Fort Nogent in the Foreign Legion Detachment in Paris (DLEP) which arranges the transit of personnel between metropolitan France and the overseas bases. The DLEP also administers the information service of the Legion in Northern France.

Following the initial selection, recruits are posted to the 4th RE at Castelnaudary. In addition to the headquarters company, there is an initial entry company; a company which trains instructors and NCOs who are also prepared for the National Military and Technical Certificates, and finally three companies of recruits. On 1 July 1984 the regiment became part of the 14th Light Armoured Division, and in June, 1985, 700 legionnaires from Castelnaudry (including the recruits) took part in a major exercise involving the 14th Division, the Milan section of the 2nd REI, Navy and Air Force personnel and helicopters of the French Navy.

Based at the Quartier Vallongue at Nîmes, the 2nd REI carries out the training of officers, NCOs and legionnaires on behalf of the GLE. Its second function is the provision of troops for overseas action, which is the responsibility of the GOLE. The regiment provides motorized infantry for the 6th Light Armoured Division, which is on standby for intervention action throughout Europe as part of the Rapid Action Force (FAR). In addition to the 2nd REI, the Legion contributes the 1st REC, the 6th REG and the 2nd REP (as an element of the 11th Parachute Division) to the FAR. The regiment's equipment consists of 20mm anti-aircraft cannons, 81 and 120mm mortars, 89mm LRAC and the Milan anti-tank rockets mentioned in the preceding paragraph. There is an establishment of eighty armoured amphibious vehicles (VABs) in different versions.

Besides the headquarters company, there is a 'recce and close support' company which has three anti-tank and two mortar sections and one intelligence section. The four combat companies also have four sections: 'Milan'; 81mm mortars: anti-aircraft; and motorized infantry. The sixth company deals with specialist instruction. In Paris on 14 July 1985 (Bastille Day) the 2nd REI (as part of the FAR) presented their colours to the President of the French Republic, during the course of a parade at which music was provided by the Legion's Musique Principale. At the same time the 1st RE and the 1st REC took part in the national festivities at Marseilles. The 3rd REI still performs the tasks described in the previous chapter, as do the DLEM and the 5th RE.

The 1st REC – which had also been known since its formation as the 'Royal' Foreign Cavalry – has an anti-tank squadron of four companies each equipped with three VABs, with HOT anti-tank missiles. Strength of the regiment is forty-five officers, 150 NCOs and 750 legionnaires, and their mobility is provided by thirty-six AMX 10-RCs and thirty-two VABs. Besides overseas participation in all types of operations, they provide European reconnaissance as part of the 1st Reconnaissance Squadron of the 6th DLB as part of the FAR which holds an annual training exercise to ensure the effectiveness of the formations. In 1985 it was known as Farfadet 1985 and took place from 3 to 7 June, involving the French Navy and Air Force, with the 4th Company of the 2nd REI which was part of a group transported by air to act as infiltrators. The first task of the 1st and 3rd Squadrons of the 1st REC (who landed with the twenty-four AMX 10-RCs that were sea-transported by the BDCs *Argens* and *Dives*) was to make a night contact with this group. The theme of this inter-service exercise was a landing from the sea in a friendly country to assist in opposing an invasion of its territory. An indication of Farfadet 85's importance may be deduced from the fact that it was attended by the French Minister of Defence, who rode for a time on board AMX 10-RC number 34.004 of Lieutenant Tatarchouk of the 1st Squadron.

Probably the best-known regiment is the 2nd REP, which has particularly high requirements for entry, even judging by Legion standards. Each company specializes in a particular skill: the first in night combat and commando; the second as mountain troops; the third special boat services and amphibious; and the fourth snipers and sabotage. Sections are made up of reconnaissance; light artillery, equipped with 20mm anti-aircraft cannons; two sections equipped with jeeps towing Milan anti-tank rockets; a section equipped with 120mm mortars towed by small LOHR specialist tractor units; and a section of skiers.

Following the establishment of the 5th RMP, a joint Legion/Army engineering unit, the 61st 'Mixed Engineers Battalion – Legion' (61st BMGL) was formed on 1 January 1971 and based at Canjours in Provence. Consisting of specialist personnel, detachments of the battalion were sent to support French units as required, but the unit was disbanded on 2 November 1982. It had its origins as the 21st Company of the 61st Batallion du Génie, which was one of the specialist units raised during the Indo-China war. However, this was not the end of the story, and on

1 July 1984, the 6th Foreign Engineering Assault Regiment (6th REG) was established, inheriting the colours and traditions of the 6th RE (the regiment of the Levant) on 12 October 1984. This specialist formation incorporates the 'Reinforced Company of Roadworks of the Foreign Legion' of the 1st RE which was based at Canjours and transferred in June 1984 to the Quartier Général Rollet at St-Morice l'Ardoise, the base of the 6th REG of which it became part on 1 July 1984. Creation of this new regiment has not, however, brought about the replacement of the company of pioneers which is an integral part of each Legion regiment.

With 700 men, it is 'an aid to mobility', building bridges, ports and other facilities and conversely the destruction of enemy mobility, in which capacity the regiment can function as a combat group. In the spring of 1985 the 6th REG visited Guyane, landing at Kourou. After a period of acclimatization, the legionnaires undertook the jungle familiarization course, after which they took part in a combat exercise with the 3rd REI before returning to France.

The regiment has its allocation of the standard Legion transport vehicles, including the VABs, all of which are 'air-portable'. Amongst its interesting specialist vehicles are three which are particularly pertinent to the regiment's task: one has the capability of carrying 448 mines (high power of destruction) and the ability to bury 330 mines per hour, notwithstanding the sensitivity of the mines. Another has high-speed mobile drilling equipment and the third is a light excavator capable of digging a trench six feet (1.8 metres deep and two feet (sixty centimetres) wide at the rate of 460 yards (420 metres) per hour.

Finally, the 13th DBLE has a company of VLRs (light reconnaissance vehicles) and twelve AMLs (armoured cars) equipped with 90mm cannons. Armaments are 81 and 120mm mortars; SS11 and Milan anti-tank missiles; LRAC 89mm anti-tank; FR-F1 snipers rifles; and FAMAS automatic rifles.

10 The Legion on Parade

Most parades are led by the band and therefore this chapter, which deals with the uniform and equipment of the Legion, is opened by the highly praised band of the Legion, the Musique Principale de la Légion Etrangère, which has a history dating back to 1831 and the formation of the Legion, whose first musicians were two buglers or drummers per company. This was quite an exceptional arrangement because the bugle was normally reserved for the elite infantry companies. However, the bugle became a vital part of the Legion's inventory in Africa, being used on the field of battle to signal 'Fix bayonets', 'Charge' and 'Cease fire'. In the barracks it was used to announce the events of the day.

Only a few months elapsed after the formation of the legion before a band was established in accordance with French Army regulations of 1827, which provided for a *sergent-major* a *sous-chef* (both ranks no longer in existence) and twenty-seven musicians. A high standard of performance was soon achieved, and by 1841, when the Legion had been divided into two regiments, the band of the 1st RE also had twenty-four singers.

A circular of 19 August 1845 revised the band establishment to twenty-seven musicians and twenty-three trainees, the command now being held in the rank of adjutant, with two sergeants and two corporals, and in 1860 Monsieur Wilhem of the 2nd RE composed the March of the Legion, '*Le Boudin*'. The status of the musicians was improved on 27 April 1889 when they became legionnaires first class and a commissioned officer took charge. In April 1902 a proper organizational structure was created with three senior ranks corresponding to the ranks of captain, lieutenant and second lieutenant, and in 1928 legionnaires in the band were given the same promotion prospects as their comrades.

In 1884 the band of the 1st RE reached a very high standard

under Monsieur Doering and at the end of 1887 an orchestra was established at Sidi-bel-Abbès under the direction of Monsieur Porch, which achieved great success and popularity. Unfortunately the outbreak of war in 1914 led to the band's being disbanded and the legionnaires taking their place in the combat regiments. After the war, Monsieur Aka re-formed both the band and the orchestra, which quickly became part of the life of Sidi-bel-Abbès, where the orchestra gave concerts on Sunday afternoons at the bandstand in the Place Carnot.

During 1929 the orchestra, accompanied by a hundred singers, undertook a tour of North Africa, the proceeds going towards the cost of building the Monument to the Dead. They participated in the celebration of the Algerian Centenary with such success that the Bey of Tunis requested the musicians to attend at his private residence, where he decorated the *chef de musique* and a number of soloists. At Sidi-bel-Abbès the musicians had another triumph at the Legion's Centenary when, on the afternoon of 30 April 1931, the orchestra and singers entertained the guests. Once again the outbreak of war, in September 1939, led to the musicians' being posted to the regiments. In 1946 the orchestra was reconstituted, to continue as one of the most celebrated military bands (whose playing gave me much pleasure one sunny autumn afternoon when I was researching for this book at the Legion's museum in Aubagne).

Although a cavalry unit was established as early as 1864, the Legion has remained primarily an infantry and construction force, strengthened by the introduction of armoured vehicles in the twenties and thirties and the formation of parachute battalions in the fifties. The equipment used and the evolution of the uniforms are subjects which justify their own individual histories and this final chapter includes only general outline. If greater detail is required, it is suggested that one or more of the books listed in the Bibliography on page 181 be consulted.

The initial armament of the Legion was the Infantry Gun of 1822, but in 1840 the Fusilide Rempart Allégé musket with sabre bayonet was issued. These weapons were gradually replaced between 1842 and 1853 by the carbine 'à Tige' percussion musket (also with sabre bayonet), the first 'rifled' version appearing in 1857, after which the earlier issues were called in for 'rifling'. At about this time the infantry companies received the 1859 carbine, called 'minie', of 17mm calibre with sabre bayonets. It was the first French Army percussion rifle used by legionnaires in the Franco-Prussian war. Towards the end of the decade, replacement commenced with issues of the 1866 Chassepot bolt-action single-shot rifle, which had the 'Yataghan' sabre bayonet. In Mexico officers were issued with an 11mm-calibre Lefaucheux revolver. On 5 March 1872 sergeant-majors lost their rifles in favour of the 1854 adjutants sabre, but in the following year adjutants and sergeant-majors were authorized to use the 1873 ordnance revolver, similar to those issued to officers. Another variant became available in 1893, and at a later date revolvers were also issued to machine-gunners.

Developments in weapons continued, and the 1874 Gras rifles which were issued for use by legionnaires were improved Chassepots, firing an 11mm cartridge, although still loading singly by means of bolt action. The need for legionnaires to carry more ammunition led to the introduction of a cartridge pouch carried across the chest, which was inspired by Colonel de Négrier. When he commanded the French expeditionary brigade to Tonkin in 1883, he ordered all his men to make pouches similar to those worn by the legionnaires. Originally known as the 'cartridge pouch de Négrier', by then it had become more usually called the 'Cartridge pouch of the Legion'.

By the mid-1890s, the Gras single-shot rifle was being progressively replaced with the new 8mm Lebel magazine rifle and bayonet with a 20-inch blade which became the standard infantry weapon until World War I, when the 07/15 and the 1916 rifles were issued to the legionnaires. In fact the 1916 Lebel carbine (and its updated versions of 1920 and 1927) lasted on in the Legion into World War II, being used at Narvik along with the MAS 36 rifles and the FM 24/29 automatic rifle (first issued in the twenties on the basis of one per platoon) – the latter in fact being used well into the Vietnam war. Another weapon used by two-man teams of legionnaires in World War I was the 1915 Chauchat 8mm automatic rifle with a semi-circular magazine holding twenty cartridges, which proved to be unreliable and was withdrawn. French rifles are referred to the year of first manufacture and the initial of the factory where they are made. These factories are located at St-Etienne, Tulle and Châtelhérault.

Returning to the Magrheb after World War I, the Legion took

with it the more modern weapons with which it had become familiar, including Hotchkiss machine-guns, and by 1937 was using Panhard AMD 165/175 TOE (exterior theatre of operations) armoured cars. During World War II, much American – and some British – equipment was issued to the Legion, and the 1st REC received American-built Greyhound M8 6 x 6 armoured cars when they entered service at the end of 1943. It carried a crew of four and had an open-top hand-traverse turret housing one 37mm gun and one co-axial ·30 inch Browning machine-gun. The regiment also received the 75mm Sherman motor howitzer carriage, and Legion units in general were re-equipped with small arms and support weapons of standard American army issue: Springfield and Garand rifles; Thompson sub-machine guns and Browning air-cooled ·30- and ·50-calibre machine-guns – the latter having a rate of fire of 450 rounds per minute – which became standard equipment; much of it was retained after the cessation of hostilities in May 1945, subsequently being used in Indo-China.

In addition to personal weapons described above, the old FM ·24/29s continued in use, but to these were added the MAT ·49 sub-machine gun; ·303 British Lee-Enfield rifles, Sten-guns and Bren machine-guns; the CR·39 folding stock derivative of the French MAS ·36 rifle and American ·30 calibre MI, and MI AI carbines. A wide variety of side-arms were carried by junior leaders until the French MAC 90 9mm automatic became standard issue. The conditions of war in Indo-China, however, led to most officers carrying carbines by 1953. Mortars of 2 inch, 81 and 61mm and the M 18 RCL 57mm recoilless rifles were of American manufacture, as were the M 29 'Crab' and 'Alligator' amphibious cargo-carriers used in Indo-China by the 1st REC, but by the time of the Suez landing in 1956 AMX13 tanks were in use. During the Algerian war British 'Ferret' armoured cars and American GMC trucks were used in addition to the French-built vehicles, but by the late sixties most of the older 'non-French' items had been replaced in the inventory by AMX tanks, EBR armoured cars and jeeps fitted with ENTAC missile-launchers. Personal weapons still included the 9mm MAT·49 sub-machine-gun which was the standard French sub-machine-gun for more than thirty years. The large variety of other weapons in use had given way to the MAS ·49/56 semi-automatic 7·5mm rifle with integral grenade-launcher, the AA·52 general-purpose machine-gun, which replaced the FM

·24/29 as the standard squad light machine-gun during the Algerian war. (The AA52 has the power to pierce 12mm of armour plating, 10cms when armour-piercing ammunition is used.) The 73mm LRAC anti-tank launcher was also used but is now being replaced by the 89mm anti-tank rocket-launcher (LRAC-Model F1) that can pierce 400mm of armour plating or 1,000mm of concrete. Although generally operated by two men, it can be operated by one.

First issued in the late seventies to the 2nd REP and the 4th RE, the weapon generally issued to legionnaires today is the 5·56mm FA MAS automatic assault rifle, which since 1980 has replaced the MAS ·49/56 and the MAT 49. Capable of firing single shots, bursts of three or continuous bursts of fire, it can also be used to fire 500-gram anti-tank rounds and anti-personnel grenades. Of particular interest is the use of plastic and fibre-glass in the construction of the weapon, which provides for the ejection of spent ammunition cases to the left or the right. In addition to the AA52 7·62mm light machine-gun, two repeating rifles (which can be fitted with telescopic sights) are in use, the 7.5mm is also available to take the 7.62mm cartridges. A re-manufactured MAS 36 bolt action rifle with ten-round magazine designated FRF·1 is issued to each of the three squad snipers in each rifle platoon.

The M621 20mm machine cannon has an electric firing mechanism and has been specially designed for use on light transporters. A multi-purpose infantry anti-tank weapon, used by the Legion either from ground or mounted on vehicles, is the Milan, which fires a missile controlled by a wire-guided remote control. It is a particularly effective weapon which has unrivalled firepower and range.

The Legion operates a wide range of vehicles ranging from Peugeot 305 cars used by the *chef de corps* through small Citroën Mehari liaison vehicles to the 16-tonne AMX-10RC armoured fighting vehicles which are equipped with a 105mm cannon and are totally amphibious. They can travel at fifty miles (80 kilometres) per hour on roads and twenty-five to thirty-two miles (forty to fifty kilometres) per hour over rough terrain. A large number of general-purpose transport vehicles are in use, but the Legion's general-purpose vehicle for combat is the Advanced Armoured Vehicle (VAB), which is amphibious and is used in numerous versions, all of which are capable of travelling for 625 miles (1,000 kilometres) without refuelling. Built by Saviem, the troop transport infantry version, for instance, carries a combat group of eleven legionnaires made up of a crew chief, driver, machine-gunner, LRAC gunner, radio operator, sniper and five grenadiers. Standard carried armament is five FAMAS assault rifles; one automatic pistol; one LRAC; an AA 52 7·62mm machine-gun and an FRF·1 sniper's rifle. The 1st REC uses the VAB in a version equipped with HOT anti-tank missiles. Specialist vehicles used by the 1st REP are jeeps used for towing Milan anti-tank rockets and small LOHR tractor units for towing 120mm mortars.

For reconnaisance the Legion uses VLRs (light reconnaissance vehicles), and another important item of equipment used in all theatres is the AML (light machine-gun) armoured car. Training on the VLR and the AML is given by the 1st REC.

Much of the equipment described in this chapter is included in the Legion's museum at Aubagne, as are the souvenirs, relics and historical items associated with the Legion. The present museum has its origins in the proposal of Colonel Wattringue, commanding officer of the 1st RE, for the establishment in 1888 of a Hall of Honour at Sidi-bel-Abbès, for display of the trophies and artefacts of the Legion. However, this did not receive universal support throughout the Legion for there were those who did not wish to part with their prized possessions, and it was not until 1892 that Colonel Zeni inaugurated the first Hall of Honour of the 1st RE. It contained the artificial wooden hand of Captain Danjou, the colour of 1871, and trophies of the battle of Tuyen-Quang. In 1903 the Hall of Honour, which was fast becoming a military museum of some importance, was visited by the President of the French Republic, Emile Loubet who commented that, 'Your museum is a museum of high patriotism in Africa.'

During the ensuing years, more and more important personalities visited the museum, and in 1931 at the time of the inauguration of the Monument to the Dead, the Temple of Heroes was established in conjunction with the Hall of Honour. Colonel Azan created a memorial Museum in 1936, and in 1938 General Catroux, commanding the 19th Army Corps, inaugurated the Hall of Battles and Flags which was destined to receive the trophies won by the Legion, their battle souvenirs and the colours of the different regiments. It was considered that the Hall of Honour of the 1st Foreign

Regiment, which had by then become a museum with four sections, the Temple of Heroes, the Hall of Command, the Little Hall and the Hall of the Battles and Flags, was an inappropriate title because the relics and souvenirs were not unique to the 1st RE but were representative of the Legion as a whole. On 30 April 1938 the inscription was changed to 'Hall of Honour of the Foreign Legion'.

In 1955 at the conclusion of the war in Indo-China, the souvenirs of this epic struggle were lodged in the Hall of Battles and Flags, which was then improved and renamed 'The Hall of Indochina' in homage to the 10,483 officers, NCOs and legionnaires who died in that campaign. Further modification took place in 1961 during the Algerian war, and a crypt was consecrated in memory of the 906 officers who died in that combat. A large Gallery of Battles was proposed but not constructed in view of the developing political situation in Algeria, which resulted in the Legion's transporting its relics for storage in the castle and chapel of the Capitain Danjou Estate in Puyloubier. The Monument to the Dead was re-erected at Aubagne in time for the Fête de Camerone on 30 April 1963. Construction of a new museum at Aubagne, close by the Monument to the Dead, was authorized in 1964 by the French Minister for the Army, and on 29 April 1966, on the eve of the ceremonies associated with the Fête de Camerone, the new Hall of Honour Museum was formally inaugurated by the veteran officers of the Legion. The author considers it an honour to have been permitted to stand on the Legion's parade ground before the Monument of the Dead.

The spirit of the Legion can be discovered by a visit to the museum, where the souvenirs, trophies and relics of the legionnaires represent their sacrifices, the meritorious acts and the glory of the foreigners who have served France for over 150 years. There are photographs, models and diagrams depicting battle scenes besides numerous paintings, photographs and other descriptive material. Part of the helicopter in which Lieutenant-Colonel Pierre Jeanpierre died is in the museum, and in the Hall of Honour are the medals of the three Hungarian warrant officers who joined the Legion in 1945, all sacrificing their lives at the age of thirty-three during the course of operations in Algeria.

Three cannons mount guard at the entrance to the museum, together with a number of armoured fighting vehicles, including a half-track, an armoured car and one of the amphibious vehicles used on the rivers in Tonkin.

The museum is located about a mile (1.6 kilometres) outside Aubagne, just off the motorway from Marseilles. Public transport is available by train from Marseilles St-Charles railway station to Aubagne station. A better way to travel is by bus service 40 from Marseilles, because not only is it more frequent than the train but there is a taxi-rank at the bus terminal, a facility not apparently available at the railway station. Opening hours for the museum are: 1 October to 31 May, Wednesday, Saturday and Sunday 10.00 hours to 12.00 hours and 14.00 hours to 18.00 hours; 1 June to 30 September, daily (except Monday) 10.00 hours to 12.00 hours and 15.00 hours to 19.00 hours.

The image most readily conjured up of the legionnaire's uniform is that of the white kepi with neck flap, white trousers and dark blue frock tunic, with the blue sash, which is still worn, as is the white kepi. The other items of uniform have long since been replaced, and today khaki or light stone-coloured uniforms are worn.

At the formation of the Legion in 1831, the uniform was based on that issued to the French line infantry, consisting of crimson trousers and a royal blue tunic, cut off straight across the waist with the tails reaching the back of the knee. Working dress consisted of a dark blue vest cut off at the waist, and in summer white trousers were issued. Headgear consisted of a dark blue shako with red top, and an 'iron-grey' greatcoat was issued. The only distinguishing mark was the button motif – a five-pointed star encircled by the unit title. In many instances, however, it was a case of being issued with what was available. NCOs wore a dark blue full-skirted coat with two rows of five buttons. By 1833 the shako had been replaced by a cap which shortly afterwards received a neck flap for protection in hot weather. All legionnaires wore moustaches, as required by the regulations of 1831, and later the tradition originated (and is still maintained) that all pioneers are bearded. In 1845 the original tunic was replaced by one cut in a style similar to a frock coat, and in 1850 the soft-topped, eye-shaded cap, in dark blue with a crimson top, replaced the 'African cap'.

When the Swiss regiment was formed, they received a green frock tunic and green vest worn with crimson trousers (although the Sharpshooters Battalion wore iron-grey trousers) and a green eye-shaded cap (referred to as the kepi, although this slang name did not come into official use until 1874). An imperial directive of 14

October 1859 suppressed the green uniform, and henceforth both regiments wore the blue and crimson, together with the kepi that had received a white cotton cover and neck flap. The present-day colours of the Legion – red and green – are derived from the Swiss experiment, and the distinctive epaulettes came into use in January 1868. As now worn, they have a green shoulderstrap with red fringes, although they have not been worn on operations since this practice was forbidden in 1881.

By May 1879 the practice of wearing crimson trousers had been reduced to winter, for parades and walking out, but in 1882 the blue waist sash became an official item of uniform, having been worn 'unofficially' for several years. It is worn over the greatcoat, tunic or with 'short-sleeve order' at ceremonial or formal occasions. Also in 1882 the white fatigue blouse was introduced for wear with the white fatigue trousers and blue sash, a form of uniform which remained until the late 1930s. Meanwhile, officers received a much darker single-breasted jacket (known as a *bourgeron*) and NCOs and legionnaires were issued in 1887 with a new-style vest. In 1893 a new dark blue tunic was authorized, and in 1899 the old-style dark blue vest was re-introduced. Uniform for officers changed again in 1895, when they received a khaki field jacket, but from 1897 officers began to wear a white field jacket. Legionnaires were authorized a dark blue tunic in 1899 for wear with both crimson and white trousers on parades and for walking out.

That most distinctive item of the legionnaire's uniform – the white kepi – originated in a cover incorporating a neck flap issued for protection against the hot sun. In 1897 the neck flap became light khaki, but soon afterwards its use diminished in the infantry companies, so much so that by 1918 it had disappeared. In mounted companies and the cavalry it remained in use until the mid-thirties, though it was not worn with the blue sash on parades, formal occasions or walking out. In 1907 the kepi cover had been changed to khaki but continuous washing and bleaching by the sun brought the colour back to white and, in so doing, provided an excellent aiming point for enemy marksmen. However, the practice continued, and on 14 July 1939, when the Legion paraded through Paris on Bastille Day, the white kepi was worn, becoming an official item which has remained synonymous with the Legion ever since. Legionnaires can now obtain – at their own expense – a purpose-made white kepi which eliminates the chore of keeping the cover white but, whereas the kepi is retained for formal wear, the green beret is worn in most situations, although in very hot climates, a light-coloured 'bush' hat with a wide brim is on issue. A not dissimilar function had been served by the khaki colonial helmet issued in 1900, in place of the earlier white version, which was worn with the 1903 light khaki French army colonial uniform first issued to legionnaires in 1909. At the turn of the century the khaki field dress gradually replaced the blue and white of the infantry, but although in fairly general use by World War I, it never wholly replaced the white fatigue field dress until the outbreak of World War II. The lightweight khaki drill colonial tunic and trousers with colonial helmet remained in use in Tonkin long after it had ceased to be worn in North Africa.

An interesting feature of Legion uniform worn in the field, which lasted until the seventies, was the '*cheich*', the muslin desert scarf. Some ten to fifteen feet long, in cold weather it gave warmth and in hot weather it gave protection for the face and head. The *fourragère* – loosely translated as a lanyard – is worn on ceremonial occasions in the manner of recognition of an award to the particular unit or regiment.

Expansion of the Legion, and the French Army in general, during World War I, resulted in the supply depots being emptied of uniforms, but by 1916 the RMLE was entirely in khaki, and for the first time a steel helmet was issued. At the end of the war surplus American Army uniforms were issued to legionnaires, and by the twenties the winter uniform was khaki tunic, *pantalon*-style trousers with puttees, double-breasted greatcoat and dark blue kepi with red top. In 1929 the French Army abandoned long-service chevrons but these have been retained by the Legion. An honour reserved to the 'head of column' of the 1st RE permitting them to wear the red and green epaulettes was extended to all units in November 1930. A major act of liberalization came in 1935 when NCOs were permitted to wear black shoes with their walking-out uniforms, and in 1938 officers were authorized a new four-button open-collar tunic. Metal unit badges of individual design, produced and paid for by the regiment, are worn on the tunic breast. The first to be issued was in 1928 to the 3rd REI; in silver and red, it bore the motto '*Legio Patria Nostra*', a lizard and a seven-flamed grenade. The practice was introduced to other Legion regiments in the thirties.

During World War II, those units raised in France were

kitted out similarly to the French Army infantry, but the 13th DBLE received the 1936-style tunic which was replaced in 1940 with British battledress, worn with the khaki beret. They later received British khaki drill uniforms and tropical helmets. In 1944 the 13th DBLE received American Army uniforms, although the kepi was retained for ceremonial purposes, a similar arrangement having applied to the RMLE and REC the previous year. Other units in North Africa tended to wear uniforms of pre-war style, although these were gradually replaced by khaki shirts and shorts. The difficulty of replacing kepis led to a side cap in regimental colours being worn, although there were some variation between the different regiments. In 1945 the RMLE 'liberated' large stocks of green ties found at a youth camp, and it became official wear in 1948.

Although there was considerable variation in the uniforms following World War II, from 1947 the 1946-style French battledress blouse and trousers were issued (worn with epaulettes and blue sash for parade and formal occasions) but in Indo-China the 2nd REI received British Army uniforms whilst American uniforms went to the 3rd REI. The kepi was retained, and side caps in red and green were worn by officers, warrant officers and senior NCOs, and in Indo-China the US MI steel helmet was issued, followed in 1950 by the green M 1946 fatigue suit. The newly formed paratroop battalions received US wartime issue Pacific theatre camouflage fatigues with the bush hat or dark green beret and the MI steel helmet which was also issued to legionnaires based in Algeria, together with the M 1946 fatigue suit worn with the white kepi. A quilted jacket-liner, together with the *cheich* and rather different, the native *djellabah* (a voluminous robe with a deep hood) all formed part of the uniform worn by legionnaires in Algeria.

In due course the American MI steel helmet was replaced by one of French design. Paratroopers received the French streaked-camouflage airborne troops' combat fatigues worn with green beret, which became standard headgear for the whole of the Legion in 1959 (as were the camouflage fatigues in 1960), the white kepi being officially reserved for walking out, parades and formal occasions. The beret cap badge is a seven-flamed grenade, although the 2nd REP is distinguished from the other regiments of the Legion by its badge, which features the winged hand-and-dagger emblem.

Parachutists wear their wings over the right-hand tunic pocket. A tunic of more modern design was issued to officers and warrant officers in 1956, but it was not until 1965 that other ranks received a four-pocket tunic worn in place of the battledress blouse and with straight trousers. There is a pale stone-coloured lightweight summer version, and officers have a white tropical service and walking-out uniform. Besides receiving the camouflage fatigues, the standard battledress and green beret, the Saharan Companies had a very special uniform consisting of the white tunic worn with many-pleated *seroual* trousers of black or white. All uniform buttons are gold except for the cavalry, which has silver.

At the time of writing a newly recruited legionnaire's initial kitting out of equipment, *le paquetage*, consists of a 'number-one uniform', shoes, ranger boots, combat clothing, shirts, green tie, overcoat, green beret, badges, epaulettes, blue waist sash and, of course, the white kepi, although this may not be worn until officially presented to the recruit. The only item a recruit is required to purchase from the mess is a first-class tracksuit, which is predominantly green with a red chevron on the chest.

Apart from medals awarded by foreign governments – for instance the 'Barretts Norvège' awarded to those from the 13th DBLE who served in Norway and the Military Bravery Cross with Palm awarded by President Mobutu of the Republic of Zaire to some of the legionnaires from the 2nd REP who 'dropped' at Kolwezi, the medals most likely to have been awarded to legionnaires are the Croix de Guerre of Foreign Theatres of War, campaign medals, the Commemorative Medal of Security Operations, and the Upholding Order (for Algeria it is worn with the clasp 'Algérie'); the wound medal; the Military Medal (awarded to NCOs and legionnaires for acts of conspicuous gallantry) and the Legion of Honour, which is the highest award which can be received for gallantry.

The Cross of Military Valour was instituted in 1956 during the Algerian war and in this instance replaced the Croix de Guerre (TOE) which could not really be awarded in a country which was at the time legally a part of France. For those who undertook ninety days on security operations the Commemorative Medal was instituted in January 1958 and, when worn with the 'Algérie' clasp, became the campaign medal of Algeria. A Colonial Medal was awarded until June 1962 but was then replaced with the Overseas

Medal, and this is also awarded with a clasp – for instance, Chad. Legionnaires who took part in the intervention in Lebanon received the same medal with the clasp 'Liban', and a recently introduced award is the 1982 Medal of National Defence. The National Order of Merit is also awarded to legionnaires.

Commissioned officers and senior NCOs (Warrant Officers) wear their rank badges in the form of stripes on their shoulder straps which all display three green chevrons and a gold grenade. On combat clothing 'velcro'd' rank badges are worn on a chest patch. The shoulderboard worn by junior NCOs has a gold grenade, whereas that for legionnaires is a green grenade, although in each case the three chevrons are green. On the left sleeve junior NCOs and legionnaires wear a shield indicating the branch of service insignia of the Legion, and in some cases this is worn by commissioned officers and senior NCOs. Ranking chevrons are worn on both upper sleeves. The metal unit insignia is attached to the right-hand breast of the uniform, usually just below the pocket flap. These unit insignia are many and varied, being issued at company and even section level.

The story of the Legion is one of continuous action and as the manuscript for this book was being completed the Legion was once again engaged in Chad. Following the intervention of French forces in 1983-4, a peace agreement was signed in November 1984 with Libya's leader, Colonel Gadaffi, as a result of which the rebel leader Goukouni Oueddi established a temporary Government of National Unity north of the fifteenth parallel cease-fire line. French forces returned to Chad soon after, when it was discovered that Libyan troops had remained in the north of the country. It was not until February 1986, however, that Libyan-backed rebels crossed the cease-fire line, to be repulsed by French ground and air forces in bitter battles on 16 February 1986, around the towns of Oum Chalouba in the north-east and Ziguey in the north-west, during the course of which French Jaguar aircraft attacked the Ouadi Doum runway using Thomson Brandt BAP100 parachute retarded/rocket boosted runway penetrator weapons. As a reprisal, a Libyan aircraft mounted an unsuccessful attack on the following day against the French air base at N'djamena airport.

The French Defence Minister, M. Quilles stated: 'France's intentions are not bellicose, but we are determined to protect Chad against aggression.' A spokesman for the rebels described the recent developments as 'French imperialism', adding that the rebels were preparing a 'final offensive' against President Habré's government.

Whatever the outcome, it seems that another chapter is likely to be added to the history of the Legion.

Appendix 1
Foreign Legion – Chronological Historical Summary

War or Campaign	Principal Units Involved	Table of Dates and Events		Killed Officers	NCOs	Legionnaires
	Old Legion	1830	Louis-Philippe becomes King of France and disbands all foreign regiments in the French Army.	—	—	—
	—		Algiers is captured by the French, and the conquest of the Maghreb begins.	—	—	—
	Old Legion	1831	Royal Ordinance of 10 March establishes the Foreign Legion and recruiting commences at depots throughout France.	—	—	—
Algeria 1832–47 (Cont'd)	Old Legion	1832	The Algerian Emir of Mascara, Abd-el-Kader, leads a revolt against the French.	27	61	756
	New Legion	1835	A new Legion is formed to fight in Algeria.	—	—	—
	New Legion	1835	Legion forces distinguish themselves at the battles of Moulay Ishmael and Macta.	—	—	—
	New Legion	1836	The new Legion arrives in Algeria and begins to train for action.	—	—	—
Spain 1835–9	Old Legion	1835	The Legion is sent to fight the Carlist army in Spain.	28	98	977
	Old Legion	1837	The old Legion suffers a heavy defeat in Spain at the Battle of Huesca in Aragon.	—	—	—

War or Campaign	Principal Units Involved	Table of Dates and Events	Officers	Killed NCOs	Legionnaires
Algeria 1832–47 (Cont'd)	Old Legion	1837 Legionnaire fights legionnaire at Barbasto.	—	—	—
	Old Legion	1838 The Old Legion in Spain is disbanded.	—	—	—
	1st & 2nd REs	1840 Royal decree of 30 December orders division of Foreign Legion into two regiments, 1st and 2nd RE.	—	—	—
	New Legion	1841 General Bugeard succeeds General Guizot as Commander-in-Chief of the French forces in the Maghreb.	—	—	—
	1st RE	1843 Sidi-bel-Abbès settled by the 1st RE.	—	—	—
	—	1844 The fort at Sidi-bel-Abbès is built by the legionnaires.	—	—	—
	1st RE	1847 The rebel leader Abd-el-Kader is captured and sent into exile in Senegal.	—	—	—
Crimea 1854–5	1st & 2nd REs	1854 The Foreign Brigade sails to the Crimea.	25	32	387
	1st & 2nd REs	1854–5 French and British troops lay siege to Sebastopol, the capital of the Crimea. 1st RE's commanding officer, Colonel Viénot killed at Sebastopol.			
Algeria 1857	1st & 2nd REs	1857 Battle of Ischeriden won by the Legion. Pacification of Algeria virtually completed.	—	—	—
Italy 1859	1st & 2nd REs	1859 Successful conclusion to the Battle of Magenta; Legion parade in Paris.	—	—	—
Mexico 1863–7	Foreign Legion Regiment	1863 Captain Danjou's unit is massacred in Mexico at the Battle of Camerone.	4	11	128
Algeria 1870	Foreign Legion Regiment	1870 Abd-el-Aziz leads a Berber revolt against the French in Algeria.	22	32	414

War or Campaign	Principal Units Involved	Table of Dates and Events	Officers	Killed NCOs	Legionnaires
France 1870–71	Foreign Legion Regiment	1870–71 Legionnaires fight in France during the Franco-Prussian War.	14	52	864
	—	1876 Death of Abd-el-Kader in exile.			
South Oran 1882–1907	Foreign Legion Regiment	1882 Legionnaires win a glorious victory over Berbers at Chotti-Tigri.	8	46	601
Indo-China 1883–5	Two Battalions	1883 A Legion battalion sails to Indo-China to help French forces fight Chinese and Thai brigands.	23	159	188
	1st Battalion	1883 Son Tay fort is captured.			
	Both Battalions	1884 Bac Ninh fort besieged by Chinese; Captain Borellis's unit captures two black flags later bequeathed to the Legion.			
	1st RE	1885 The conquest of Indo-China completed by the French	—	—	—
Formosa 1885		1885	3	6	24
Dahomey 1892–4	One Battalion	1892 Legionnaires in action in Dahomey.	2	4	31
Sudan 1893–4	Detachment	1893 Operations in the area of Kayes and Timbuktu.	—	—	2
Madagascar 1895–1901	1st RE	1895 Expedition to Madagascar.	5	27	228
Morocco 1907–14	2nd RE	1907 France establishes protectorate in Morocco.	5	21	229
	—	1908 Death of the Berber leader, Abd-el-Aziz.			
	—	1912 Treaty of Fez.			
Morocco 1914–18	1st RE	1914 Abd-el-Krim and the Riffs rise in revolt against the French in Morocco.	4	40	304

War or Campaign	Principal Units Involved	Table of Dates and Events	Officers	Killed NCOs	Legionnaires
France 1914–18	RMLE (one battalion) (Middle East)	1914–18 World War I, legionnaires fight in the trenches of France, Gallipoli and the Dardanelles.	155	42	4,349 (all theatres of war)
Russia 1918	Battalion	1918 Legion fights against Bolsheviks in northern Russia		No details available	
Tonkin 1914–40	5th RE from 1930	1919 Syria becomes a French protectorate. 1920 Legion withdraws from Tonkin for a short period in 1919–20	1	5	49
Syria 1925–7	1st RE	1921 1st Foreign Cavalry Regiment is formed. 1925 Druze warriors revolt in Syria.	2	6	37
Morocco 1920–35	2nd, 3rd, 4th REs	1926 The Riffs revolt is finally crushed.	74	158	1,264
France 1939–45	11th & 12th RE 21st, 22nd & 23rd RMVE 13th DBLE	1931 Centenary of the Legion. 1939 World War II breaks out in Europe.	— 118	— 821	— 8,078
	13th DBLE	1940 Legion forces withdraw from Norway. France is conquered by the Germans. Marshal Pétain agrees to co-operate with the Germans and Hitler. General de Gaulle forms the Free French Army in Britain. 13th DBLE arrives in Britain from France.	—	—	—
	13th DBLE/6th REI	1941 Free French legionnaires of the 13th DBLE clash with legionnaires of the 6th REI loyal to Pétain in Syria.	—	—	—

War or Campaign	Principal Units Involved	Table of Dates and Events	Killed Officers	Killed NCOs	Killed Legionnaires
	13th DBLE	1942 Epic defence of Bir Hakeim.	—	—	—
	1st REIM	1943 Legion fights with the Allies in Tunisia.	—	—	—
	13th DBLE, 1st REC & RMLE	1944 Legion fights in Italy and then lands in France.	—	—	—
		1945 End of World War II.			
Indo-China 1946–54	2nd, 3rd & 5th REIs, 13th DBLE, 1st REC, 1st & 2nd BEP	1947 Legion units sail to Indo-China to re-establish French control.	309	1,082	9,092
		1947 Vietnamese war starts.	—	—	—
		1954 The French Army is defeated by the Vietnamese at Dien Bien Phu.	—	—	—
Madagascar 1947–50	Battalion of 4th DBLE	Legion spends further period in Madagascar.	3	1	1
Algeria 1954–62	1st RE, 2nd, 3rd, 4th & 5th REIs, 13th DBLE, 1st & 2nd REC, 1st & 2nd BEP (later REP) Sahara Companies	— Algerian rebels rise in revolt against the French.	63	264	1,528
Tunisia 1952—4	2nd REI		2	1	11
Algeria 1955	1st & 2nd REP	1955 Two Legion parachute regiments are formed.	—	—	—

War or Campaign	Principal Units Involved	Table of Dates and Events	Killed		
			Officers	NCOs	Legionnaires
Morocco 1953–6	4th REI Sahara Companies	1956 Morocco and Tunisia become independent states.	3	7	56
Egypt 1956	1st REP & 2nd REC	1956 Anglo-French landings in Egypt (Suez Canal).	—	—	2
Algeria 1958–62	—	1958 General de Gaulle is made President of France and promises Algeria independence.	(casualties shown Algeria 1954–62)		
	1st REP	1961 French Army units in Algeria, including the 1st REP, rebel against de Gaulle. The 1st REP is disbanded.			
		1962 Algeria becomes independent, and Legion units leave the Maghreb. The Foreign Legion is reorganized.	—	—	—
Djibouti 1963 to present	13th DBLE	1963 onwards Legion forms garrison.	—	—	—
Chad 1969–70	2nd REP	1969–71 The 2nd REP and a Composite Motor Company are sent to restore order in Chad, in central Africa.	—	—	7
Zaire 1978	2nd REP	1978 The Legion rescues Europeans in Kolwezi.	1	—	7
Chad 1978–9	2nd REI 1st REC	1978–80 Renewed disorder in Chad brought the return of the Legion – this time contingents of the 1st REC and the 2nd REI.	—	1	4
Lebanon 1983	2nd REP, 2nd REI 1st REC, 1st RE	1982–3 Legionnaires form part of the multi-national peace-keeping force in Beirut in the Lebanon.	—	—	1
			—	—	5

War or Campaign	Principal Units Involved	Table of Dates and Events	Killed		
			Officers	NCOs	Legionnaires
Chad 1983–4	1st REC 2nd REP	1983–4 Further trouble in Chad causes the Legion to be deployed there for a third time.	—	—	—

Note: 1st RE retains title as such, but 2nd, 3rd, 4th and 5th REs were subsequently redesignated Foreign Infantry Regiments, i.e. 2nd, 3rd, 4th and 5th REIs.

Appendix 2 The Account of the Battle of Camerone

As read annually on 30 April by the President of the British ex-Foreign Legionnaires Association to the members at a parade in London.

On 29 April 1863 Colonel Jeanningros asked Captain Danjou to organize a company as escort to a major convoy leaving Vera-Cruz for Puebla. It was the 3rd Company's duty tour but, noting that all its officers were sick, Danjou proposed that he should command it. To assist him in this task, he took the standard bearer, Second Lieutenant Maudet, and the paymaster, Second Lieutenant Vilain.

The column left at one o'clock in the morning on 30 April, intending initially to reach Palo-Verde. Meanwhile the Mexicans, having learnt of the passage of the convoy, organized a force of 800 cavalry and three battalions of infantry – about 2,000 all told – to attack it.

At about 05.00 Danjou's company stopped for a brief halt and, having posted sentries, set about making the morning coffee, which was well under way when the sentries announced approaching cavalry. In seconds the coffee was thrown away, the mules were re-loaded and the company was moving to the outskirts of the village of Camerone – whence rang out the first shot of the battle, that of a nervous Mexican sentry. The first cavalry charge quickly followed and was as quickly broken up and repulsed by well-controlled fire and by the use of the thick scrub into which Danjou had moved his force. In the hubbub the mules took fright, broke loose and disappeared with the rations, water and spare ammunition. The sixty-five-strong company had but sixty rounds apiece. Danjou decided to stand and fight and to engage the enemy, thus distracting their attention from the valuable convoy, and rapidly moved his force into a defensive position in the nearby *hacienda*, where they were to hold for the next ten hours. By nine o'clock the sun was already high – the legionnaires had no water, no food. Colonel Millan commanding the Mexicans called on the legionnaires to surrender – they replied that they had ammunition and had no intention of surrendering. The legionnaires promised Danjou that, come what may, they would fight to the bitter end. He was killed at about eleven o'clock. At this moment, the three battalions of Mexican infantry arrived on the scene, and again the legionnaires were called upon to surrender. They replied '*Merde*'. The situation worsened – the Mexicans had broken into various rooms of the *hacienda* and, having killed the legionnaire occupants, had set fire to the rooms. For the wounded – intense heat, dust, smoke and no water. The battle continued – Vilain was killed just before 2 p.m. and Maudet took command, but by five o'clock he had only twelve men in a state fit to fight.

Again Millan called on the legionnaires to surrender – they did not deign to reply – and a fresh attack was launched against them; Maudet was now alone with a corporal (Maine) and four legionnaires (Leonhard, Catteau, Wenzel and Constantin). Their *cartonchieres* were empty – they fired a final salvo and leaving their shelter charged the Mexicans with their bayonets – all fell before reaching them. Maudet received two bullets. Legionnaire Catteau, who had thrown himself in front of his officer to protect him, was hit nineteen times. They were the last. It was 6 p.m. and the battle was over. Maine, Wenzel and Constantin, although wounded, were still standing. Of the sixty-five-strong company, two officers and twenty-two legionnaires were dead, one officer and eight men mortally wounded and nineteen soon died of their wounds in captivity; twelve others, all wounded, were captured.

When Maine, Wenzel and Constantin were called upon to surrender, they said that they would not do so unless they were allowed to keep their arms and tend their wounded; Colonel Millan said, 'One can refuse nothing to men like you.'

The Mexicans lost more than 500. The Emperor Napoleon III had the title 'Camerone 1863' inscribed on the banners of the 1st Regiment; and in 1892 on the site of the battle, a monument was raised on which is inscribed:

ILS FURENT ICI MOINS DE SOIXANTE
OPPOSES A TOUTE UNE ARMEE
SA MASSE LES ECRASA
LA VIE PLUTOT QUE LE COURAGE
ABANDONNA CES SOLDATS FRANCAIS
LE 30 AVRIL 1863

[Here stood fewer than sixty men against an entire army. Its weight overwhelmed them. Life, sooner than courage forsook these soldiers of France. 30 April 1863.]

Appendix 3 Organization

Table of Comparative Ranks (a)

British	French	American
Field Marshal	*Maréchal de France*	General of the Army
General	*Général d'Armée*	General
Lieutenant-General	*Général de Corps d'Armée*	Lieutenant-General
Major-General	*Général de Division*	Major-General
Brigadier	*Général de Brigade*	Brigadier-General
Colonel	*Colonel*	Colonel
Lieutenant-Colonel	*Lieutenant-Colonel*	Lieutenant-Colonel
Major	*Commandant*	*Major*
Captain	*Capitaine*	Captain
Lieutenant	*Lieutenant*	First Lieutenant
Second Lieutenant	*Sous-Lieutenant*	Second Lieutenant
–	*Aspirant*	–
–	*Major*	–
Warrant Officer 1	*Adjudant-chef*	Chief Warrant Officer
Warrant Officer 2	*Adjudant*	Warrant Officer Junior Grade
–	*Sergent-Major* (obsolete)	First Sergeant
Staff Sergeant	*Sergent-Chef*	Master Sergeant
–	–	Sergeant First Class
Sergeant	*Sergent* (b)	Sergeant
–	*Caporal-chef*	–
Corporal	*Caporal* (c)	Corporal
Lance-Corporal	*Soldat (légionnaire) de 1re classe*	Private First Class
Private	*Soldat (légionnaire) de 2e classe*	Private

Notes

(a) Exact equivalents do not necessarily apply.
(b) '*Maréchal des logis*' is used in the French cavalry instead of '*Sergent*'.
(c) '*Brigadier*' is used in the French cavalry instead of '*Caporal*'.

Recruiting Centres
STRASBOURG – Quartier Lecourbe
MARSEILLES – Bas Fort St-Nicholas
PARIS   – (Fortenay-sous-Bois) Fort de Nogent (also the
                      base of the Détachement de Légion Etrangère
                      de Paris which administers information
                      centres in northern France)

Appendix 4 Glossary

Arab	A native of North Africa or the Middle East
Aurès	Mountain range in Algeria; a treeless wilderness
AWOL	Absent without leave
Bataillon de marche	A special unit made up of experienced legionnaires
Battalion	Unit formation between 500 and 800 legionnaires
Bey	Turkish word used to describe the ruler or governor of a town
Bled	French Army name for the outback
Cafard	The mythical 'black beetle' which legionnaires claim invades their minds in times of stress
Caid	Arab local governor; an honorary title by which Legion senior officers were known in the twenties
Colon	European settler
Corvée	Fatigues – menial tasks awarded to junior soldiers
Djebel	Mountain
Fellagha	Arab guerrilla
Foreign Brigade	A unit of two or three Legion regiments serving together away from North Africa
Jihad	Holy War
Katiba	FLN company
Kepi	White uniform cap worn by legionnaires
Magrheb	('Land of the setting sun') Tunisia, Algeria and Morocco
Mechta	Neighbourhood of a village
Oasis	Fertile area in the middle of the desert
Pied Noir	'Black Foot' – European settler in Algeria
Regiment	Army unit made up of about four battalions
Regiment de marche	Experienced legionnaires assembled for a special task
Riff	An inhabitant of the Atlas mountains in Morocco
Ultras	Diehard *pied noir* conservatives, resisting all change
Voltiguer	Elite infantryman
Wilaya	One of the six FLN commands in Algeria

Appendix 5 Foreign Legion Regiments and Companies

In the text, the English version was given, with initials (in parentheses) taken from the French form. Below LE = Légion Etrangère = Foreign Legion.

French initials	French form	English form
BEP	Bataillon Etrangère de Parachutistes	Foreign Parachute Battalion
BMG-L	Bataillon Mixte Génie-Légion	Mixed Legion Engineering Battalion
CCS	Compagnie de Commandement et des Services	Headquarters Company
CEA	Compagnie d'Eclairage et Appui	Reconnaissance and Support Company
CEV	Compagnie d'Engagés Volontaires	Recruits Company
CIC	Compagnie d'Instruction et des Cadres	Instruction and Cadres Company
CMMLE	Compagnie Mixte Mortier de la Légion Etrangère	Foreign Legion Mixed Mortar Company
CSPL	Compagnies Sahariennes Portée de la Légion	Saharan Motorized Companies
CRTRLE	Compagnie Renforcée de Travaux Routiers de la LE	Reinforced Road Building Company of the FL
CTLE	Compagnie de Transport de la LE	FL Transit Company
DBLE	Demi-brigade de Type Montagne de la LE	FL (Mountain) Half-brigade (later FL half-brigade)
DIMa	Division Infanterie de Marine	Marine Infantry Division
DLEM	Détachement de LE de Mayotte	FL detachment of Mayotte
DLEP	Détachement de la LE de Paris	Paris Detachment, FL
FAR	Force d'Action Rapide	Rapid Action Force
GALE	Groupement Autonome de la LE	Autonomous Group of the FL
GCP	Groupement Compagnie Portée	Motorized Company Group

French initials	French form	English form
GERD	Groupe de Reconnaissance Divisionnaire	Foreign Divisional Reconnaissance Group
GLE	Groupement de LE	Foreign Legion Group
GOLE	Groupement Operationelle de la LE	Operational Group of the FL
GPLEM	Groupement Portée de la LE du Maroc	Motorized Group of the FL, Morocco
ITLE	Inspecteur Technique de la LE	Technical Inspector of the FL
REC	Régiment Etranger de Cavalerie	Foreign Cavalry Regiment
REG	Régiment Etranger de Génie	Foreign Engineering Regiment
REI	Régiment Etranger d'Infanterie	Foreign Infantry Regiment
REP	Régiment Etranger de Parachutistes	Foreign Parachute Regiment
REIM	Régiment Etranger d'Infanterie de Marche	Foreign Infantry Marching Regiment
RILE	Régiment d'Instruction de la LE	Foreign Legion Instruction Regiment
RMA	Régiment de Marche* d'Afrique	Marching Regiment, Africa
RMLE	Régiment de Marche de la LE	Foreign Legion Marching Regiment
RMLE-EO	Régiment de Marche de la LE – Extrème Orient	Foreign Legion Marching Regiment – Far East
RMP	Régiment Mixte de Pacifique	Mixed Pacific Regiment
RMVE	Régiment de Marche de Volontaires Etrangères	Marching Regiment of Foreign Volunteers

* See Appendix 4 for connotation of *régiment de marche* etc.

Bibliography

The Eighth Army, September 1941 to January 1943 (HMSO, London 1944)
* *Uniforms of the French Foreign Legion 1831-1981*, Martin Windrow (Blandford Press Ltd, 1981)
History of the Second World War (Purnell & Sons Ltd, 1966)
The French Foreign Legion, John Robert Young (Thames & Hudson Ltd, 1984)
The French Foreign Legion, Nigel Thomas (Sentinel book published by Wayland Ltd, 1973)
The Dammed Die Hard, Hugh McLeave (Saxon House, 1974)
Strange Company, Adrian Liddell Hart (Weidenfeld & Nicolson, 1953)
Daily Mail (25 September 1984)
The Most Important Country – the true story of the Suez Crisis, John Connell (Cassell & Company Ltd, 1957)
Suez 1956: Operation Musketeer, Robert Jackson (Ian Allen Ltd, 1980)
Report of the Committee of Enquiry into Events in Bizerta, Tunisia 18-24 July 1961 (International Commission of Jurists, Geneva, 1961)
In Lightest Africa, H.T. Kenny (John Murray, 1935)
A Savage War of Peace, Algeria 1954-62, Alistair Horne (Macmillan London Ltd, 1977)
Devil's Guard, George Robert Elford (New English Library, 1972)
Legionnaire, Simon Murray (Sedgwick & Jackson, 1978)
The French Foreign Legion, Erwan Bergot (Allan Wingate (Publishers) Ltd, 1975)
A Modern History of Somalia, I.M. Lewis (Longman Group Ltd, 1980)
Mutiny 1917, John Williams (William Heinemann Ltd, 1962)
L'Épopée Moderne de la Légion 1940-1976 (Société de Production Litteraire, 1977)
Livre d'Or de la Légion (1831-1981) (Charles-Lavauzelle, Paris & Limoges, 1981)
La Légion, Pierre Sergent (1985)
French Foreign Legion Paratroops, Martin Windrow and Wayne Braby (Osprey Publishing Ltd, 1985)
Armies in Lebanon, 1982-84, Samuel M. Katz and Lee E. Russell (Osprey Publishing Ltd, 1985)
* *Képi Blanc* – various (Service Information et Historique de la Légion Etrangère)

181

Operation Epaulard 1 Beyrouth, Eric Lefèvre (Charles Lavauzelle, Paris and Limoges, 1982)

＊ *The Battle of Dien Bien Phu*, Jules Roy (Carroll & Graf edition, New York, 1984)

＊*French Foreign Legion Mines and Booby Traps*, (Paladin Press, Boulder, Colorado, 1985)

Index